A CONVERSATION
BETWEEN THE BROTHERS

Written by Tracy Elaine (Robinson) Humphrey

Beginning of Writing: October 23, 2020

Completion of Writing: December 2, 2020

A Conversation Between The Brothers © 2022 by **Tracy E. Robinson Humphrey.**

All rights reserved. This book or any portion thereof may not be reproduced or used in any manner whatsoever without the express written permission of the author except for the use of brief quotations in a book review. Printed in the United States of America.

First Printing
ISBN# 978-1-955148-28-3 pbk
ISBN # 978-1-955148-33-7 ebk

A2ZBooks Publishing Lithonia, GA 30058 www.A2ZBooksPublishing. net. Manufactured in the United States of America A2Z Books Publishing has allowed this work to remain exactly as the author intended, verbatim.

FOREWORD

How do you deal with the harsh realities of racism? Do you merely listen to the news reports, register anger, join demonstrations or just wait for justice to happen? Or should you do as Tracy Humphrey has done—take pencil to paper to express her feelings about the outrageous acts of racism.

In A CONVERSATION BETWEEN THE BROTHERS, Tracy Humphrey writes the stories of the African American males who were killed by racist white cops. She describes how they are then welcomed into the University (Heaven) by the Master (the Creator) who welcomes them back with open arms, but also recognizes that they are returning home, all too soon.

Author Humphrey has chosen a poetic way of handling a very sensitive topic—the tragic demise of six African American males who were killed by white racist cops. Her style of writing weaves through narrative and rhyme, a unique way of telling their stories —stories that are very different from those reported by the media at the time of their killings. These brothers, as she refers to them, were killed because they were black.

We are introduced in the beginning to Amadou Diallo the first brother to arrive at the University (Heaven). As the first, he becomes the designated one to acclimate the other brothers to their Home. Upon arrival, each receives a tour of their "Mansion"-- a place that resonated with their earthly existence. The brothers arrival is heard through the sound of chimes—which heralds the welcoming of succeeding brothers killed by the white racist cops. They wait in anticipation for the sound to see who is coming next. However, as the brothers navigate through the University, they notice chariots. These chariots are only used by the Master who goes to receive those who are sick and ready to come to the University.

Tracy Humphrey has the brothers tell their truly agonizing stories through a variety of strategies like the Name Game, rhyme/rap, heartfelt interaction and fellowship. Her ability to convey the dignity of these brothers shines a light on the value of their lives.

There is a mix of the spiritual and the secular in telling their stories. As I read the book, I couldn't help but think that this is a form of a parable—an earthly story with a heavenly meaning. As a Christian it is comforting to read about the brothers who were killed being welcomed into the University (Heaven). Tracy Humphrey has transformed the inhumanity they experienced on earth to a profoundly humanizing experience in the University.

Dr. Nettie Webb

CONTENTS

ACKNOWLEDGEMENT 1

CHAPTER 1 10
   The Introduction

CHAPTER 2 17
   The Untimely Arrival of Two

CHAPTER 3 20
   Together Forever We'll Be

CHAPTER 4 25
   Music of Afar

CHAPTER 5 29
   Trayvon Gets the Tour

CHAPTER 6 35
   The Very First Supper With the Master

CHAPTER 7 38
   Racist Cops Didn't Let Us Stay

CHAPTER 8 40
   Their Own Deaths They Could Not Avoid

CHAPTER 9 47
   Was It Fake Or Were They Mistaken?

CHAPTER 10 54
   Screaming For Her After the Chase

CHAPTER 11 56
    The Brothers Start To Get Down
CHAPTER 12 63
    From The Bottom, But to The Top
CHAPTER 13 65
    I Thought I Knew You Then
CHAPTER 14 69
    Music In the Air
CHAPTER 15 72
    Annoyed Or Overjoyed?
CHAPTER 16 75
    After He Remembers That Time
CHAPTER 17 82
    The Master Told Them He Was Nice
CHAPTER 18 92
    It's Better Out Than In
CHAPTER 19 102
    Don't Believe What You Heard

Acknowledgement

First and foremost I must thank THE ONE who has entrusted me with HIS gift of writing. Without HIM I am nothing and can do nothing: My Lord and Savior, JESUS CHRIST. HE gets all of the credit for this book. I am just a vessel HE used for such a time as this. I'd also like to thank the following people: Mrs. Briana LaTruth (for putting me in touch with your Publisher), my College English Professor (Dr. Penelope Prentice) for her last words to me: "Whatever you do in life, don't stop writing", Sis. Eartha B. Williams for giving me my first experience at writing for the public via "The Eye On Calvary Newsletter", my biggest cheerleader since the age of thirteen and the best Brother n' Love I could have ever asked for; The late Stephen E. Fraley, my Bestie who has been pushing me to write a book since 1980; Dawn NB (inside joke for "Tinks") Barrett; (I love you, now get off my back), Sean Barrett, 'Londa" Barrett, Dr. Christina Gorman (for her great photography, and for keeping my eyes healthy), my "Neighborhood Mayor"; JoEllen Gorman, my friend since third grade; Yvonne "Best Friend" Hammonds (I love you bunches), my BFF Kathy (John) Cambriello, Carol Bretones, Lenny Sanders, my "Little "D" (Aunt Tracy loves you so much!), my MEMA (Dora Ragin); I love you and your cooking so much, our family, friends, and Godparents to our Tony; Bruce and Irma Edington (we love you), Pastor Rick and Executive Pastor Deidra "Dee"

Boreland (we love you to life!), Pastor Ray and The Living Word Christian Church family, Elders Gerry and Debbie Matts, Sandra Dennis, Angie Bilotta, Minister Aaron Kelly (faithful, and genuine friend; I love you so much), James (Buster) Baker (for your prayers and for receiving me as your sister), Pastor Daryl and First Lady Tanya Young, (I love you. Keep the JOY in JOY CITY!). My hairstylist; Leasa Pemberton (you are the best and I love you just because you're you).

I'd also like to acknowledge other family and friends who may or may not know that they are dear to my heart (*PLEASE KNOW THAT THIS LIST COULD NOT BE EXHAUSTED): My Cousins: Lisa B., Rene, Judy, Robin, Paula, Sonya, Denise, Torre, Jason, and "Cousin Jeremiah CJ". My friends: Anne Tacoma, Jeff "Jeffie" Zitofsky, "Matt the Man" Seidlinger, Sheller (Brunson) Edwards, Barbara Dubois, Linda Washington, Mechelle Rooke, Charlene (Mickens) Toliver, Deneen (Mickens) Canty, Ademola Adeyeni, Michael and Jennifer Soravilla, Azetta Ayanruoh, Camille Spaulding, Nikki (Ephraim) Corbin, Sandy (Gina) Goodman, Amy "Ames" Heffernan (I love you), Rochelle Herring, Amy Moran, Irene Lum Cheong, Christina Lett, Kenneth Chamberlain, Jr., Leonard Johnson, Latoya "Greenie" Robinson, Ali Morgan, Apostle Harry Dawkins, III (and wife, Prophetess Sondra Dawkins), Janet Kennerly, Vincent and Kim Cioce, The late Mr. Thomas and Mrs. Mary Rutledge and family, Dr. Selena "Birdie" Pitt, Michael and Chrissy Tetro, "POP-POP" Moccia, Arlene-Grace Staples, Wilma Houston, Darlene "Doll" Boney, Margaret Turner, Isabell

Burrows, Dr. Celina Ponce, Elizabeth Hall and "The Peekskill Five" (Wayne, Parker, Greg, Jared, and "Rich").

I must acknowledge some of my family who have transitioned: "Granddady" (Lawrence Williams, Sr.), "Gramma" (Connie Mae Williams), Father n' Love who was the best. I love and miss him every single day (Fred Humphrey), "Grandma" in' Love (Elizabeth Hall), my favorite cousin EVER; (Karen Denise (Robinson)) and Cousin Stanley "Sir Jello Shot" (Inside joke) Hall. My Uncles: (Reverend Lawrence "Larry" Williams, Lawrence Robinson, James "Jim" Williams, L.C. Williams, James "Bubba" Williams, Uncle James "Sonny" Hall. Eddie Robinson, Howard Robinson, and Jerome Long). My Aunts: (Gladys Bryant, Sarah Williams, Great Aunt Jewel, Grace Washington, Diane Robinson, and Frieda Hall).

I acknowledge my nephews (Keith, Terrell, Jamel), nieces (Tammy, Marthia, Antonia, Lydia, Jasmin, Kelsey, Montana, Miyah), great nieces (Brittany, Jordyn, "Charley", Ayana), great nephews ("CJ", Logan), my great great niece (Zare'uh), my Uncles (Reverend William Smith, Curtis Robinson, Steven Robinson), Aunts (Mary Robinson, Jerry Robinson, Brenda Robinson, Joyce Long, Joyce Smith, Estelle Holt, Ann Rogers, Effie Smith and Brenda Young-Marbury), my College family (Darlene Young (I love you BUNCHES);, Belinda Simmons, Deacon Allen Knight, Sr., and Mother Claudette Knight (and family), and Mother Joyce Glenn and family). I have an extensive list of cousins and I love them all. However, there are several cousins who may or may not know that they are dear to my heart: Linda B., Rene, Judy, Robin, Joan, Paula,

"CJ Jeremiah", Jason, Torre, Monique, Pastor Gene, Denise, and "Sonya Girl".

I have to thank the loving family given to me by God: To my Mommy (Imani Bolling), God has blessed me with you because He knew I needed a "Mommy". To thank you for all you've done (and continue to do) for me and for the way you love me would take another book! There are no words that can describe how very much I love you. Thank you for rescuing me, helping me to find myself and for accepting me as I was and am. I don't know what this world would be like without you in it. There is NOTHING I wouldn't do for you. Your heart is made of pure gold and I'm blessed to be in its midst. In the words of BeBe Winans: "FOREVER IS A LONG TIME AND THAT'S HOW LONG I'LL LOVE YOU"! To my Auntie Gail Bolling, and Cousin Zuleka DeGrace, I love you.

To my Daddy (Tony Robinson): There's not a day that goes by that I don't love you, think about you, and miss you. Thank you for allowing me to be a daddy's girl. I know you're in a MUCH BETTER place, and if you had the choice, you would not want to return. However, the selfish part of me wants you here with me! A piece of my "puzzled heart" will always be missing because you carried it with you when God called you home. It comforts me to know that when it's my turn to come, you will once again make my heart complete. I wish Heaven had visiting hours. If it gets crowded up there, save a seat for your "Tray"! As you always said, "I'll be eyeballing for you"!

To my brothers whom I love with all of my heart: Steven "Skeeter" Robinson (also God Father to our Greyson); it only takes three words to describe you: SIMPLY THE BEST", Lester G. Cousin, Anthony "Allen" Robinson (if I searched the world over and over, I know I'd never find a brother as great as you), and Bruce "Brucie" Robinson (I love you and thank God that you're my brother. Your heart is huge and loving. Thank you for all the laughs while growing up. I know you love me too, "Dancing Machine"). To my late brother; Leonard "Moe" Wilkins: I still can't believe you're gone! I miss you every minute of every day. There will never be a Coach or Line Dancer better than you! Thank you for teaching me how to do "The Wobble" and for loving (as you would always call them), "My Boys"!

To an awesome and caring team who I thank for keeping me healthy in more ways than one and for fixing pieces of me that you had no part in breaking. Without a doubt, God led me to you because He loves me just that much: Dr. Silvio Burcescu and Dr. Debbie Lang. The two of you never cease to amaze me with your well rounded intellect. Thank you for saving me from myself and from others. Tex and Didley, I love you too!

To my sisters who I love and who will always have a home in my heart: Jennifer "Gem" Slade (ME AND YOU, US NEVA PART. I love you beyond measure), Jacky Wilkins (God showed out when he put us together), "Big Sis" Angela (Cousin) Carter (we will ride together until the wheels fall off, and even then, we'll buy a new car!), my "Bigger Big Sister"; Rhonda Robinson (I love you and the strength within you; Crystal Smith (Love you much)...; Patricia Fraley there is not a better sister (or Aunt to "Your Boys") than you anywhere on this Earth. Time will not permit me to share how much I love you. Please continue to make me laugh until I cry, can't catch my breath, and my stomach hurts. Being with you is ALWAYS a good time and as you say, "No fool, no fun". You've NEVER met a stranger. God did me a solid when He gave me you for a big sister. I could never thank Him enough. I love you to the moon and back one million times. Make sure you never take in strays (inside joke)!

To my loving husband (The Honorable Judge Wayne A. Humphrey): You are second to NONE! Babe, I cannot thank you enough for loving me unconditionally while treating me like your queen, best friend, lady of your life, and soulmate. Thank you for putting up with my baggage of "stuff" and for helping me to unpack it. You love me deep and respect me as a woman to no end. You are the most caring and selfless person I know (and it doesn't hurt that you do well at spoiling me). God could not have given our sons a better Dad. They simply love and adore you. You continue to do a phenomenal job at being the man and head of our household. You work hard to provide for our family and I hope you know how much we love and appreciate you. You and I make a great team. Our sons have never wanted for anything and it's great to see that they are happy, well spoken, intelligent and motivated. I am thankful to you for so many things and reasons. I can happily and truthfully say that there is nothing I need or want. You make me happy and you complete me just by being Wayne. I'm blessed to get to spend forever with you!

To my Mother n' LOVE, Eva Smith: You are living proof that a woman can love and have a great relationship with her daughter n' law. I love the time we spend together and for all the laughs. Thank you for raising A GREAT MAN and for being proud and supportive of your grandsons. We love you tremendously.

To my late Father n' LOVE, Fred Humphrey: I love and miss you so very much. Thank you for always loving and accepting me as the only daughter you had. It's still hard for me to look at the chair that was "Papa's Chair, or the upstairs bedroom that was Papa's (and Mama's) bedroom. You'd be so proud of your grandsons, but I know you're cheering for them from the stands of Heaven. Rest well and easy, Papa!

To my sons (Greyson Tyler Humphrey and Tony Robinson Humphrey): I love you more than anything. From the moment you entered this world you have been and continue to be my pride and joy. There's nothing I wouldn't do for you. Thank you for always being leaders and learning that loving yourselves as you are is more than enough. You have always astonished me with your brilliance, even when you were toddlers. You should be proud of yourselves for all that you have accomplished thus far. I know you'll go further and I can't wait to see what the both of you will contribute to the world. I'm grateful that you've always (and continue to) hear me tell you how much I love you AND BELIEVE IT! Thank you for loving me back. Continue to set high goals and work hard to reach them. The University of Southern California and Boston

College will be even better because each of you have graced their campuses with your presence. Always love each other and remember to keep God first in your lives. He is always just a prayer away and His Angels will surround you every day of your lives. Remember the last words PaPa spoke to us before he transitioned: "Have a nice life. And have a good life. You too Tracy; have a good life". We've been doing it. Let's continue to do it and make PaPa smile with pride in Heaven. I am proud that you remember (and do) what my Daddy (and your Grandaddy; Tony Robinson) taught me to do: "Save. If you make a dollar, save fifty cents, if you make fifty cents, save a quarter, if you make a quarter, save a dime". I love you both more than you'll ever know and there's nothing you could do or say to ever make that change or stop.

To the man who will ALWAYS be my Pastor; Dr. Reverend Lester Cousin. I love you for so many reasons, but to sum it up: As a shepherd you've always allowed me to be your sheep AND MORE! I will always love and respect you. To my "MaMa" (Mary) Cousin; I love you so much! You have always been a Proverbs 31 Woman. There is nothing I wouldn't do for the both of you!

Finally, to the families of the victims represented in this book, if "justice" has yet to be given to you, I hope and pray it's on its way. Yet, I can only imagine how painful your hearts will always be because the only REAL JUSTICE would be to have your sons returned to you. It is said that time heals wounds. If this is so, I hope time is moving swiftly for all of you. I hope the world will NEVER forget your sons. I know

I won't! My prayers will continually go up for you. Be blessed and as much as possible, be at peace.

T.E.H.

The Introduction

With skin like bronze and eyes of brown, He also had a wide nose. He could have worn an afro or fade, but it was locs He chose. With many jeans, shirts, and robes, He was most comfortable in his dashiki. Because His streets and floors were made of gold, His Jordans didn't sound squeaky. The Master looked around with sweat on His brow, pleased at what He created. He knew that when His sons returned from earth, they really would be elated. Thinking of a name for His masterpiece, He finally decided on "The University". He never told them how they'd return, but they'd be at peace without adversity. The Master tossed his locs back; they hung almost passed His chin. He walked to the window and pulled back the curtain to see the souls He'd save from sin. The University had many mansions and one could easily get lost. The Master knew when His sons returned, the rent would be no cost. He already had many other children there whose returns were not yet supposed to be. Most returned by racist cops; George Floyd in 2020 by a left knee. The Master loved all His children, He made them to be kind and nice. He saw these attributes in all of His children; especially

Tamir Rice. Tamir was just a baby at twelve, enjoying Chicago's recreation center. There he made embroidery for his mom and he even had a mentor. He acted like the boy he was; playing outside with friends and his "Cuz". One of his favorite toys was his airsoft gun; everyone knew it was fake. He never knew that playing with it would cause his deadly mistake. In that same year there was Eric Garner who they accused of selling Loosies or cigarettes that are single. Just as with George, when he was being killed, a concerned crowd began to mingle. Eric was loving, kind, humble, and yes, he was also bold. But that doesn't mean he should have returned home by the cops' illegal chokehold. He said he was tired of being harassed and that the Loosies weren't sold by him. The Master thought, "Why did they do that to my son? They accosted him on a whim". Still in that year of 2014 Michael Brown Jr. was another one to arrive. Michael was only eighteen years young, and he had the will to thrive. He could have made it in the music industry, having his own business gig. Like his brother Eric, "Big Mike" returned home because of smokes. At this point the Master began to think, "These cops are killing my sons as if their lives are jokes". "Big Mike" graduated from high school, and was sent home eight days later. Had these racist cops left him alone, I'm sure his life would've been greater. Even with his hands in the air and yelling " I don't have a gun", they pumped at least sixteen bullets into his chest as if he was nobody's son. Conversing with Himself, the Master said, "Racist cops must believe that killing blacks is cool. Two days after they murdered my son, he was scheduled to begin college school. There's also something interesting about my sons I see. I know that I am the Master of all, but even I am baffled that this could be". Michael and his brother Eric were sent home with no more goodbyes or hellos. Each of them because of smokes; Loosies and cigarillos. They claimed "Big Mike" stole them from a nearby convenience store. Even if he did, this does not equate his life being no more. Darren Wilson didn't just kill Michael, even though his life was plenty. This racist cop wasn't charged in the death according to the courts in 2020. The Master sat at His table sipping Petrone which helped Him to inspire. After a while He knew what He'd do; He'd create a Dump House with a lake of fire. It would be the forever home for a murderer, a racist, and a liar. Each mansion in the university started to fill with the Master's unexpected sons. The Master noticed that many of them were sent home by racist cops' guns. Just two years after "Big Mike" was sent home, the Master's son Ahmad Aubrey came. At this point even the brothers agreed that racists thought they were playing a game. On earth, Ahmad was minding his own business while running through a wealthy neighborhood. A white man and his son followed him in their truck with guns just because they could. At the age of twenty-five, if left alive, he knew his life would have thrived. Instead, the racists cut his life short and that's why he arrived. The white man and his son confronted him and asked him why he was running through the neighborhood. I can imagine young Ahmad thinking like them; "simply because I could." But he didn't say a word because he was unarmed and saw that they each had a gun. He must've thought to himself, "I'm dead if I stand here and I'm also dead if I run". He saw the son's gun rise and point towards his face. Then all he remembered was whispering, "I'm saved by my Daddy's grace." So,

Ahmad joined his brothers when he entered the gates which were so beautiful and pearly. The Master met him once he was in, hugged him, and said, "You're home early". Ahmad replied "I thought I was, but at least here I'll be safe. Sometimes on earth, I really felt as if I was a waif". The Master began to explain to him that he bled out after he was shot. He never rode in an ambulance because he was dead on the spot. The Master said He was glad he was home, but the racist father and son would pay. He showed him the lake of fire he made for them when they came to him one day. One by one the sons arrived home early not knowing that the others were there. Each could only stop in his tracks when seeing the others and stare. Now in the year of 2012, the month of February to be exact. Another one of the Master's sons was senselessly attacked. Trayvon Martin was sent home early twenty-one days after turning seventeen. The way he was sent was not only racist, but cold, calculated, evil, and mean. In a townhouse community he was visiting his father and his dad's soon to be wife. The farthest thing from his mind was that someone would end his life. Hoodie over his head, girlfriend on his cell, and skittles in his hand, he was just returning from the store. Trayvon became a bit concerned when he heard the slam of a car door. He told his girlfriend he thought there was someone following him from behind. So, he knew he had to become more vigilant because the back of his head was blind. He started to check his surroundings on both sides and in the rear. At first, he was cool because he didn't see anyone but then he heard steps coming near. He knew he had to pick up his pace; it was getting dark and he started to fear. Suddenly a white man approached to ask him what he was doing in the neighborhood. Trayvon asked the racist why he was following him, and he stopped walking and stood. What he didn't know was that the racist had already called 911. But Trayvon also didn't know that the Master would be greeting yet another son. The racist reported to the operator that he saw a suspicious person. He was instructed to stay in his truck and not to approach him; it may make things worsen. But the racist coward carrying a gun acted like a vigilante. That he in fact did not remain in his truck, the operator couldn't see. With his head held high, he told Trayvon that he was Captain Watch for the neighborhood. Twice Trayvon screamed for help in hopes that someone would. His girlfriend stayed on the phone with him but then she heard the phone drop. Trayvon cried for help twice, then the Watchman's bullets began to fly. The neighbors in the community heard so many shots that they were certain someone would die. White hoodie still over his head, and his cell phone near his chest, Trayvon's left hand was open where his unopened skittles were at rest. When Trayvon was sent back home, the Master again shook his head in disbelief. "Another racist sending home my son for me to hide my grief". February 4, 1999 had the Master crying this time. His son Amadou Diallo was walking down the path and the Master made the welcome bell chime. Before Amadou could enjoy his home, he had to deal with the flashes playing in his head. He did briefly notice the Master releasing the many tears He shed. Amadou focused on the trauma in his head which he'd work to somehow heal. He didn't yet want a welcome home tour nor a meal. The fog and anxiety in his head were the first thing he had to cure. He started with the memory of coming to the USA to live the American dream. He never forgot the first hot day when he tried Carvel ice cream. His thoughts jumped to the incident that occurred outside the building where he called home. He knew that the first officer who approached him could never be his gnome. Holding his doggie bag from the restaurant where he ate, Amadou Diallo imagined that the morning would be great. Although his stomach was full, his body was tired from working all day. He and his cousin had a business selling merchandise on the street 'cause they had bills to pay. At approximately 12:40 in the morning, Amadou saw four plainclothes cops in a car that slowly drove by. The four white officers stared at him as if he'd done something bad. But because he was such a positive young man, he thought, "maybe someone made them mad". Just in case they asked him for his ID, Amadou took his wallet out. Then the four racist cops jumped out of the car running towards the Master's son, Amadou. He didn't know what was happening, so he started running too. A chase ensued near the building resided by Amadou Diallo. He took a look back as he was running and saw that the cops were slow. Amadou knew that he ran faster because he knew the way. But regardless of tha, he remembered thinking that on earth he'd no longer stay. As he remembered being chased, he knew that was no fun at all. He had so much pain in his head, it felt like it was hitting against the wall. He could still hear the shots going off and he counted them in his head. Pow, pow, pow, bang, bang, bang; to the tune of forty-one. He saw one of the four cops trip on a stair and he fell back. He hoped he hit his head and black out so the Racist Four would lack. Instead, the bullets seemed to come faster and he could still feel the sting and the pain. With every shot, his body being tossed, he prayed that the shots would wane. The racist cops used semi automatic pistols and began shooting without any warning. Many were awakened by the gunshots, after all it was 12:40 in the morning. When the Malay was finally over, Amadou laid motionless on the ground. The residents and other bystanders prayed that cops wouldn't shoot another round. The racist cops tried to block the crowd from seeing what they already saw: Four plainclothes racist white cops kill another black man who didn't even break a law. There were no weapons seen around Amadou's body by the now larger crowd who decided they would stand. The one and only object they saw was Amadou's wallet, innocently resting in his hand. When they saw the cops' semi-automatic pistols, all they could do was stare. Pistols versus a wallet? They knew this "occurrence" wasn't fair. About Amadou's life, the racist four didn't care. Now that Amadou defeated his flashes, his mind was clear and he could proceed. He saw a brown skinned man wearing a familiar Kango hat and thought, "Yup, that's the Master indeed". With his headache gone, Amadou walked faster and then he started to run. He knew the Master loved him and he knew that he was His son. Through the pearly gate, another black man entered, sent home too soon by a racist cop of white. Nevertheless, Amadou knew that from that night he'd be alright. An early welcome home from the Master, with a needed hug for a while. Amadou recognized the oil on His neck and remembered it was called Blue Nile. The Master explained to His son that he wasn't supposed to be back home yet. But each agreed even if that was the case, they were happy that again they'd met.

END OF CHAPTER 1

The Untimely Arrival of Two

(Trayvon and Amadou)

Tipsy from what may have been too much Hennessey, the Master planned to lay down. But before He went to His mansion, he noticed Amadou's face wearing a slight frown. The Master lovingly told him that he would not be alone. "What do you mean?" asked Amadou; the first of the sons to arrive. The Master explained that there would be another brother who was not permitted to stay alive. He explained to him that he'd have to be the one to welcome his first brother when he came. "But I never met him" Amadou replied. "I won't even know his name". With a tight hug given to His son, the Master told him not to be afraid. He can first start by telling him about his time on earth and all the friends he made. He said he'd have on jeans, skittles in his left hand, and a white hoodie over his head. He also may be tired from the journey, so the Master showed Amadou his bed. "Promise I can find you if I get stuck on what to say". "I promise you I will", the Master said, and he showed him the mansion where he'd lay. So Amadou stood at the gate, waiting for his brother to arrive. In due time he knew he'd ask him who didn't let him stay alive. Before he knew it he saw a young boy who appeared even younger than he. As the youngster got closer to him, Amadou thought "this can't be who I see". Then he remembered the Master telling him how his outfit would be. Without initially seeing the jeans nor the skittles in his left hand, Amadou saw the hoodie over his head and thought, "This must be my brother I see". Nervously and slowly Amadou opened the pearly gate. The time had come to meet and greet his brother and he didn't want to wait. The young boy in the hoodie with his left hand closed slowly proceeded towards the gate. He saw the young brown man standing there reaching out his opened and welcoming hand. He started to jog but then he ran while the hoodie fell from his head. He wasn't sure who was welcoming and greeting him but he hoped he had a bed. When reaching the open gate, the older man held the younger. Although they had never met, each felt as though they'd love the other. Amadou introduced himself to his brother and he asked him for his name. The stranger within the younger boy replied, "I'm Trayvon Martin and the way I was sent home was a shame". He said he'd tell him all about it later, but right now he was tired and only wanted a bed. Amadou showed Trayvon where his very own mansion stood. He assured him he'd be safe if he decided to wear his sweatshirt with the hood. Just as the others Amadou saw, Trayvon's mansion was huge and brightened by the sun. In amazement Trayvon asked how he'd be safe because he never used a gun. Amadou explained that the University was totally safe and he'd have a lot of fun. "I know you're tired", Amadou said, "so I'll let you sleep Little Brother." He felt that he wanted to hug him tight, but Trayvon he didn't want to smother. As he turned to walk away, Amadou realized that his pace was a lot faster. But he stopped, looked behind him, and said to Trayvon,"Tomorrow you will meet the Master".

END OF CHAPTER 2

Together Forever We'll Be

(Watching a Movie by The Great Spike Lee)

Trayvon awakened well rested but still he laid in bed. He wanted to think about what got him there but he toured his mansion instead. He was extremely impressed by all he saw, but he still wasn't sure if he was dead. He finally found the kitchen in his mansion with food and drinks galore. Trayvon happily thought to himself, "I'll never again have to visit the store". Just then he remembered that he had fallen asleep with his skittles still in his left hand. But now it didn't matter to him, for he had his own Candyland. A table held many bags of skittles on his left and he noticed a new cell phone on his right. In shock he saw and read the sticker "You may call your girlfriend tonight". He thought he remembered her cell phone number but then again he wasn't certain. "I know her number" he heard a voice say, and he knew it came from behind the curtain. Trayvon glanced towards the curtain which was now pulled back halfway. The tall brown man caused Trayvon to whisper, "This will be a great day". Somehow he realized that this man was responsible for his beautiful abode. Last night he had secured his mansion, so he thought this man had the code. He stood against the wall which held the curtain and crossed his arms against His chest. For some reason Trayvon thought to himself, "I think this place will be the best". Never saying a word, the man remained in his position now wearing a grin. It seemed he intentionally posed this way so that Trayvon could take his appearance in. Needless to say Trayvon was shocked and yes, he was in awe. A man with features just like his dad's is what he thought he saw. Blinking his eyes and shaking his head to make sure his mind was clear, Trayvon read about this man while on earth and he remembered what clothing he would wear. There could be no doubt in his mind who this man had to be. There was also no doubt about him knowing only one way this man he'd be able to see. In a very faint whisper, Trayvon asked himself, "Am I now dead"? The man smiled, chuckled, and whispered back, "Son, I heard what you just said. Your brother will be here soon and we'll sit at my table and talk. Then afterwards there will be some time for the two of you to take a walk. I want the two of you to get to know each other and to learn how much you are the same. I also want you to talk about how your murderers thought killing you was a game". At this time the man slowly walked towards Trayvon with his arms wide open to receive. Once Trayvon got a closer look at his clothes, what he saw he just could not believe. The man continued to slowly walk towards him as Trayvon took in his brown and flawless skin. With his very own mansion, with a Candyland, he thought, "This place is a win-win". Inspired by the man's outfit,

Trayvon's feet were locked in their place. The man wore a black and white Adidas sweatsuit and the matching Adidas Boost were on his feet. The only thing the two of them could do was stare into each other's face.. Trayvon remembered Amadou telling him that he'd meet the Master today. And as he thought he was doing it now, Trayvon didn't know what he should say. Instead he wanted to prepare himself for the walk with Amadou that day. Walking closer to Trayvon, the man began to smile. He wanted to be certain Trayvon was comfortable, after all he'd be staying there for a while. He held His arms out wide, ready to hug his son. Trayvon entered the arms of the man who said, "Your race has now been run". Trayvon felt comfortable in the arms of the stranger, even though he knew not who He was. He thought the man could have been his pastor and instantly he heard, "Welcome back home son, I am the Master". Trayvon released his neck from the Master's and recognized his scent; African musk. Immediately he knew his brother would teach him so much more and he wanted to start before dusk. As if the Master read his mind, He took his hand saying, "Let's go find your brother, as I told the both of you, I want you to love and get to know each other. Trayvon and the Master found Amadou in the theater watching "Do The Right Thing" by Spike Lee. Trayvon immediately sat next to him watching a large screen he could easily see. He glanced back to look at The Master who wore a smile on his face. He put one hand on each of their shoulders and said, " I'll give you brothers some space". Almost simultaneously, the brothers watched The Master walk away. Although each didn't know it, they both wanted Him to stay. Suddenly, The Master turned back around and said to His sons, " Don't forget to take that walk. It's important that you get to know as much about each other as possible; your brothers and you need to talk. Trayvon and Amadou promised they would as soon as the movie was done. Amadou was confident that the walk would be a lot of fun. The Master told His sons that He would talk with them if there was time when they got back. If they were tired upon their return, it would be fine for them to hit the sack. The Master knew that He'd have forever to explain to the brothers why they were there and would never go back. The brothers continued to watch Spike's movie and took a break during the intermission. The snack room outside of the theater held foods only for great nutrition. There was a table already set with fruits of different kinds. The brothers had everything they could think of, so much so it blew their minds. Both were glad there was no watermelon; that fruit they never cared for. Grapes, blueberries, cantaloupe, pineapple; those fruits they loved and more. Plates, utensils, and napkins were all prepared with class they'd never seen before. Every fruit they each loved as well as smoothies in a diamond glass. Frozen yogurt from a platinum dispenser, they couldn't decide which flavor to choose. But without a doubt, whatever the flavor, they knew they could not lose. But then they told each other why vanilla they wouldn't choose. They found one thing in common; the white caused them their lives to lose. In shock, the brothers stared at each other and their words escaped them fast. For the very first time in the University, the brothers got a clear glimpse of their past. As Amadou chewed coconut, Trayvon chewed blueberries as if they were skittles so sweet. He said to his brother, "I can't wait to tell you why I'm here". "Me neither" Amadou said, "But, the movie's restarting, so let's go grab a seat". Feeling more comfortable with each other, the Brothers talked through the show from Spike. As they listened to the songs, they each imagined their boys back home; killing it with the mic. They remembered all the songs from the movie, and every one they could name. Amadou thought of a way they'd get to know more about each other via a game. He explained to his little brother that they could play that game. "Since we know that we're brothers and here is where we belong, let's get to know each other from Spike's movie by using the appropriate song". Trayvon didn't understand what his big brother was saying, so he asked, "can you break that down for me?" " I'll give you an example little brother, but you have to listen to me closely. Can you do that for me, little brother? Can you do that for me, Tray"? "I think I can, big brother Amadou, yes I know I can". And this is when Amadou smiled, and it's where his game began.

END OF CHAPTER 3

Music of Afar

(Do The Right Thing and Jekalyn Carr)

"I think I was killed, but it's HARD TO SAY. I know I was made to cower. I had no chance against the four white cops; they were racists and I couldn't FIGHT THE POWER. Trayvon's face looked as if it shined, and he told his brother his game was one-of-a-kind. "Your turn now Tray, lemme hear whatcha got". Then Trayvon started sharing his story right on the spot. "I know I was young, but marrying my girl was still MY FANTASY. I knew I belonged in my dad's neighborhood, but the racist white man said, "PROVE TO ME". "Ayee, you got it little brother, you killed that one Tray. OK it's my turn again, I got some more to say. I was being chased by four racist cops and to this day I don't know why. Many blacks and whites couldn't get along and as I was running I thought, "WHY DON'T WE TRY"? I ran as fast as I could, sometimes dodging a small tree. In my head I spoke to the four racist cops, "please, please, "DON'T SHOOT ME". When the four racist cops were chasing me with their guns, I really didn't "FEEL SO

GOOD". I remembered however that it wasn't the first time racist cops murdered in my neighborhood. With that in my head and at the same time running, I whispered to myself "I CAN'T STAND IT"! That was around the time when so many shots rang out that my neighborhood looked lit. I guess the racist cops shot me, I was motionless on the ground. With my wallet in my hand and my face looking above, the last words I remembered came from the voice of a man saying "racist cops could 'NEVER EXPLAIN LOVE'!". The brothers gave each other a pound and they playfully punched each other's chest. Amadou said, "I don't miss earth", and Tray responded, "Me neither; up here we are blessed". Before they knew it, the credits on the screen had started rolling. Amadou said they didn't have to stop talking; they could catch up in the north wing where they would be bowling. He explained to his little brother that the north wing was too far away for them to get there by feet. He saw the question in the eyes of his brother's, so he answered, "The Master has drivers and a fleet". Looking relieved, Trayvon asked Amadou if he could show him where. Amadou responded, "Sure, it's in this direction"; he pointed and said "right over there". Trayvon's eyes changed, appearing as large as the bowling balls they'd soon hold. He couldn't believe the size of the fleet, and the beautiful cars parked on streets of gold. "Yooooo Bruh, whose cars are these? I'd like to ride in a Porsche, but then again the Lamborghini is faster". "There's no rush" Amadou replied; "all these cars belong to The Master. We'll be here forever and the cars will too; besides there's so much more to do". Trayvon looked past the first fleet of cars until he saw another. In awe he asked, "If this is the fleet here, then what's over there big brother"?

Amadou explained that the other fleet held chariots from which they could never pick. "Only The Master rides in them when He travels to earth to bring home the sick". Seemingly having a swift understanding, Trayvon turned his head back around. Still in disbelief, he was mesmerized by the bright and glistening gold ground. "Pick any one you want Tray, either is fine with me. Like I said we can ride them all 'cause we're here for eternity". There were so many cars in so many colors, so The Master gave each a number. A driver stood tall next to the car he was responsible for. It seemed like forever, but Trayvon approached the stretch Lamborghini and the driver opened the door. He was followed by his big brother, and he knew no racist would hurt him anymore. The ride to the bowling alley wasn't very close; they'd have a two hour drive. Amadou and Trayvon didn't mind; they were just grateful to again feel alive. Amadou told his little brother that there was an Alexa in every car. He said The Master put them in for them because they traveled so far. Trayvon asked if the machine would play any songs he'd like. Amadou explained that it would and he showed him how the volume could spike. "I wanna hear my favorite singer; Evangelist Jekalyn Carr". "OK little brother, get comfortable." "I am". "You sure you are"? Trayvon nodded his head and Alexa was instructed by Amadou to shuffle songs by Jekalyn Carr. Trayvon asked his big brother if they could again play his "Get to know me game", since the ride would be so long. "No problem", Amadou said, "But I bet you know every song". Trayvon smiled as if he was busted, but said he wanted to go first. And amazingly on cue, the first song began and Alexa's volume burst. Amadou commanded Alexa to turn the volume down and she adhered so very well. Then Trayvon anxiously began the personal story which he now wanted to tell.

END OF CHAPTER 4

Trayvon Gets the Tour

(That's What Big Brother is For)

"I was returning from the store. I was alone 'cause I was NOT TOO YOUNG. Wearing my true religion jeans with my hoodie over my head, it felt like spring had sprung. I needed to be back home by seven, 'cause I made that PROMISE to my Dad. IN THIS ATMOSPHERE, I was on my cell with my girl, talking 'bout what I WANNA BE. I was only seventeen, so I didn't really know; I had time for my destiny to come to me. I couldn't wait to open my skittles which I carried in my left hand. I reminded my girl that I loved her and that together WE WILL STAND. She agreed because we loved each other, so she said to me "Trayvon, WE ARE ONE. I smiled into my cell and replied "Baby, YOU WILL WIN" 'cause I am ONE WITH YOU too. My girl would always ask me, "What would I do without you Boo"? I'd always say "Baby, don't worry about that; I BELONG TO YOU too. Out of nowhere I heard a car door slam. For some reason, when I was walking,

A CONVERSATION BETWEEN THE BROTHERS

I felt like I was NEVER ALONE. A white man approached me and asked what I was doing in that neighborhood. I asked him why he was following me and for him to explain if he could. He said he was the neighborhood's Watchman, and then I saw the gun which held his finger on the trigger. With the only weapon being my skittles, I wanted to tell him YOU'RE BIGGER". "Why are you walking here?" he asked "this isn't your neighborhood". Knowing nothing good would come from me running, I nervously stayed where I stood. In my head I told myself, "Trayvon, STAY RIGHT HERE". In my right ear my girl was yelling, "Trayvon, what's wrong? Who is that bothering you"? "I'm okay" I said; 'cause there was nothing else I could say or do. He obviously thought he owned the neighborhood. "If you spare my life", I wanted to tell him, "This neighborhood? "IT'S YOURS!" The evil look in the racist man's eyes spoke to mine saying "BIGGER IS COMING!" Bracing myself for what I knew was true, I nervously squeezed the bag of skittles in my left hand. I wondered once he shot me, "where would my body land?" Telling myself, "IT'S GONNA HAPPEN", I screamed "help"; not once but twice. I saw the flashes of light from the gun and then I felt the bullet's pain. I remember thinking to myself, "This racist must be insane". I remembered hearing myself in my head telling my girl, "BRING ME BACK TO YOU". I knew I certainly was not the first young black boy to die, and I always wondered why racist individuals never cared about the YOUNG PEOPLES' CRY! After I saw where my body landed, everything went dark for me. I felt someone lift my body from the ground and hold me as if I was a baby. I knew it was a man, but I didn't know who. The racist man, a racist cop, or even my dad maybe. As soon as my body was touched by this man all of my pain went away. Although I didn't know this man, in his arms I wanted to stay. My eyes saw the light even though they were closed still. "Am I dead?", I wondered to myself. "And if I am, was it all God's will"? It seemed as if the bright light was medicine for my eyes. With the warmth on my face, I opened them thinking, "My how time flies". Before I even looked at the man, I knew I was being taken somewhere. He placed my body in something that could fly; just like the chariot back there". Trayvon stopped talking and inquisitively looked at Amadou's face. "Was The Master the one who came for me and drove me to this place"? "No little brother, you were not sick; the Racist Watchman" sent you back. Remember? You didn't do anything wrong Tray. He murdered you 'cause you were black". They both agreed that it was all good and that the University was GONNA BE GREAT! "We are now OVERCOMERS" said Amadou with his new brain. "Now that you're living here Little Brother, YOU WON'T SEE THE WIND OR THE RAIN". Trayvon looked at his brother and in his head he counted from one to three. "You greeted me at the gate when I came, and "YOU SPOKE OVER ME". "Yes I did Tray. Although like me, you returned too soon, your Homecoming was SOMETHING BIG"! "The Master is so down to earth, you'd never know He suffered loss". Amadou responded, "The Master gave His life for us when He willingly died ON THE CROSS. Get ready little brother, the bowling alley is just to the right. We can't stay very long because the Master wants to have dinner with us tonight". The brothers talked as they bowled and they each felt so connected. Somehow they knew that in their new home they would never again be rejected. Amadou quizzed Trayvon on African American Men who bowled. "Nah man, nah man, no; that's something I was never told". "There are two of them", Amadou said "and neither was very old". With Trayvon being totally blank, Amadou told him that one was George Branham the third. "Yo, Big Brother, lemme find out you smart. George Brandom the third? Say 'word'". Amadou admitted that he only gained such knowledge since the day he entered the pearly gate. "STAY WITH ME" he said, "the learning here is always great. All of the ANGELS GONE BEFORE YOU left their education for the others to come. That's why African-Americans are extremely smart; even though we were often seen as dumb". With his final strike, Amadou threw his hands up shouting "I AM A WINNER"! He told Trayvon they could get another game in before it was time for dinner. Ignoring what he said, Trayvon asked, Big Brother, have you ever been a sinner?" "Everyone is born into sin, that's just something that they do. But like us, they only have to repent and say, 'LORD I LOVE YOU'. Then The Master will hear them, forgive their sins and again receive them home". "Well, I sure am glad that The Master saved me 'cause so many people on earth would just roam". "Yea, me too Little Brother; me too. Without salvation I know I wouldn't be here, I'd be living in the Lake Of Fire". "What? A Lake of Fire? "Big Brother, what do you mean"? Amadou told him about the lake the Master created; that lake that he had seen. "Why did He make a "Lake Of Fire" when we have cool oceans and rivers to see"? Amadou explained to Trayvon; "The Lake Of Fire" was made for murderers and liars, not for the Repenters like you and me". "Big Brother? Would you do me a favor? Would you hug me and HOLD ME CLOSE?" Amadou took his little brother into his arms and held him close after kissing his nose. "I love you Little Brother" he said, "Just wait and you will see". "I believe you, Big Brother, 'cause already I LOVE THE WAY YOU LOVE me". Reluctantly letting his little brother leave his arms, Amadou pointed to the alley and said, Come on Tray, let's get one more in." Trayvon waved his hand at his brother and said, "Nah man, you know you'd win". "Aight then Bruh, let's take this ride back, we got dinner and The Master to see". Walking side-by-side, Trayvon looked up at Amadou and said, "Big Brother? Thanks for greeting me." Holding back the tears in his eyes, he noticed Tray's facial expression was flat. So he nudged his little brother on his shoulder saying, "Come on man, you know you got that." With a smile returning to his face, Trayvon said, "Big Brother, let's do something. Let's see who has the fastest run." "Nah Bruh, my knees are bad; I'll give you that right now". Trayvon started running anyway and when his brother caught up he wondered how. The brothers were exhausted from running but they were proud that they were able. Once they each caught their breath Amadou said, "Let's go have dinner with The Master at His table." Once in the car and happy to have learned Alexa, Trayvon commanded her to again play Jekalyn Carr. "It's your turn this time" he said to Amadou, "It's your turn to play the game." Amadou looked at Tray like he was buggin' saying, "You used every song and every name. There aren't any left for me." "Actually Big Brother, you used some yourself; let's listen to the shuffle and you will see. So the brothers laid back comfortably, and they both listened to

Evangelist Carr. Both ended up taking a nap, knowing that the mansions were pretty far. Each of them had their own peaceful dream about how great their lives would be. And each wondered if it would just be them or would there be others to see.

END OF CHAPTER 5

The Very First Supper With the Master

(Drinking From A Glass Made of Alabaster)

Awakened by the driver and finally arriving home for dinner, Amadou and Trayvon each thought how grateful they were for no longer being a sinner. They knew The Master was waiting for them in His own mansion to have dinner at His table. Amadou hoped he'd remember the tour The Master gave him so that he'd know which one was His. Trayvon hadn't yet gotten the full tour, so Amadou said to himself, "He wouldn't know where it is". Amadou remembered that it wasn't too far from the pearly gate. The driver would have told them to continue the ride so that they wouldn't be late. Amadou remembered the quick rap he made in order to remember the way: "The Master is the best and His mansion's in the west". He sang this rhyme loud enough for Trayvon to hear. He looked up at his brother's face and thought he saw confidence there. Amadou explained why he was quickly rapping with his words sounding like a song. He explained that if he did this, they'd be at The Master's mansion before too long. Trayvon immediately joined his brother in this rapping song. In his mind he trusted his brother and he thought he could do no wrong. Amadou's destination seemed to now be clear. He saw The Master sitting on His porch nursing a bottle of beer. As they got closer, Amadou mentioned that he smelled another one of The Master's body oils; frankincense and myrrh. Remembering the scent on the neck of his Dad, Trayvon said to Amado, "Big Brother, I concur". As they continued to walk closer to the mansion, The Master stood up to welcome them another time. As if on cue, the brothers eyeballed the corona on the table, its neck holding sliced lime. Trayvon wanted to ask his brother about this, but decided to do it at another time. The brothers folded comfortably; both in the Master's arms. Jokingly The Master looked at His sons and said, "I was just about to have my posse send out the searching alarms". "Come on in", The Master said as He held the platinum gate for His sons. There was a delicious smell of familiarity which the brothers recognized as hot cross buns. In awe of The Master's mansion, they were there to eat and greet. Seemingly jarring them back to the present, The Master said, "Let's gather at my table and eat". Each of the brothers turned around his body, and lastly he did his head. Yet again they were flabbergasted. They saw before them a long diamond table with a spread. They wondered if it was Thanksgiving in the University, but to ask, they had no will. The Master already told them that in the University, time stood still. Every day will be every day and every night every night. Viewing the confusion on the faces of His sons, The Master said, "Don't worry, soon you'll get it right." Amadou and Trayvon's eyes scanned the table;

the amount of food they could not believe. Just as they prepared to say Grace, twice they heard the scream of "I can't breathe." The brothers looked at The Master for an explanation of the same scream with two different male voices. Before He pushed back from the table He said, "More racist cops just made deadly choices". He told them that He had to welcome two more of His sons at the gate. He admonished them to start eating, so the brothers very slowly ate. Never had they tasted food this delicious, so their fingers they began to lick. "Will you be driving the chariot down to meet your next two sons"? "No Trayvon, just like the two of you, My sons coming back home were not sick." Amadou said, "I thought I explained it to you, Little Brother. Remember? We were in the lot." "Oh yeah, my fault, my bad Big Brother; with all of the excitement I forgot." Removing the unused satin napkin from His knee, The Master carefully sat it near his plate. Once again He told His sons He'd return, but He had to rush so He wouldn't be late. As they continued to eat, the brothers each wondered: "Who could be waiting at the gate?"

END OF CHAPTER 6

Racist Cops Didn't Let Us Stay

(They Took Our Breath Away)

The Master hurriedly walked to His bedroom, and inside His walk-in closet He now stood. He had to decide which outfit to change into. This was His custom, so He was confident He would. Although He again was not expecting His sons, He was aware that when they arrived their lives would be new. So in a symbolic gesture, The Master made sure that each of His outfits were too. Still in a hurry, He decided on a white and gold Gucci top. Rushing as he stepped his legs into the matching pants, He wondered if the racist officers were several or just one cop. Lastly, He slipped His feet into His gold and white kicks made by Kobe Bryant from the Lakers. He knew He would now be comfortable when he greeted the racists' dead makers. "Who will they be this time?" he wondered. "Who's given my sons an untimely return home now"? Were His babies again killed by racists for nothing? If so, He wondered how. As The Master glided down the very long hallway, the gold floors again glistened and shined. He knew He wouldn't have early greetings if the racist cops would just be kind. The closer He got to the gate, The Master began to feel nervous. He wondered which of His children this time had been given a disservice. As was now His custom, The Master approached and opened the pearly gate's window to view. His mouth opened in disbelief when He saw not one son, but two. As the brothers walked towards the gate, they moved their necks from side to side. Each had their own story to tell, but the physical pain they wanted to hide. Even far from the distance, The Master saw that the young men breathed with trouble. This was not the case for just a single man, but for the double. The Master sensed that this was the case, but knew they'd feel fine once they entered in. Within the University, they'd know no pain nor sin. Finally, the brothers reached the now opened gate and dropped at The Master's feet. They recognized Him right away and knew their return would be sweet. The brothers had already been introduced to each other by their families on earth. Unfortunately, each of them learned that to racist cops, they had no worth. With pain in His heart and tears in His eyes, The Master had to do what He couldn't avoid. He opened the gate to welcome His sons; Eric Garner and George Floyd.

END OF CHAPTER 7

Their Own Deaths They Could Not Avoid

("I Can't Breathe" said Eric Garner and George Floyd)

The Master held His hands downward to bring His sons up from the gold and glistening ground. Although their return to the University was too soon, He knew it would be great having them around. His younger sons would now lovingly have two big brothers with them forever. The love and bond they'd share, no racist would ever again be able to sever. Eric and George would come to know that the University held only peace and joy. The family would see each of them as a great man, and not as a racist's little nigger boy. The Master embraced both His sons together; George on His left and Eric on His right. The tighter He embraced them, the more He noticed that their breathing was quickly becoming normal. At the same time, the intense pain left their necks and somehow they knew they'd now be immortal. When released from the Master, George felt his nose for blood and the right corner of his mouth for foam. When he found that his face was dry, he tearfully yelled, "Momma, I'm home!" The Master explained to George that his Momma was waiting for him to return. But because he returned home too soon, He'd have to prepare her to learn. He explained to George that he had his very own mansion and that his Momma did as well. This is why she'd never hear him if he'd decided he wanted to yell. He informed both His sons that they had two younger brothers who they'd be elated to see. He told them that they were in time for dinner; He reached out his hand and said, "follow me." Eric and George walked with the Master, each on one side. As they did, they took in the beauty within the University and wondered if it was there that they'd reside. They each got a feeling that never again would there be a racist cop to force them to take another "squad car ride". After the fairly long walk to The Master's dining room, the older sons saw two boys eating at a table. Realizing that they must be their younger brothers, Eric felt excited while George's legs felt unstable. Amadou and Trayvon remained seated for another introduction to their big brothers of two. Both were shocked at their sizes and thought, "What did they NOT do?" This time it was Tray who wanted to initiate Amadou's name game. Because they appeared much older, he didn't think their stories could be the same. The Master knew the older brothers must've been hungry, so he invited them to sit and eat. He excused Himself before encouraging the brothers to have more meet and greets. Amadou saw what looked like a raindrop fall from the Master's eye landing on his Kobe sneaks. The Master silently wondered when others of His children would return too soon. But every day was every day, so he wouldn't know if it would be days or weeks. Before again admonishing the brothers to love one

A CONVERSATION BETWEEN THE BROTHERS

another, The Master turned and walked away. Feeling as if the "crying mucus" was suffocating Him, He could form no other words to say. Uncomfortably sitting at the table, the four brothers thought each seemed nice. Yet not one of them seemed bold enough to speak and break the ice. Suddenly, being the man that he was, Eric said, "well, I'm Eric; I guess I'll start". He told his brothers to come closer around the table so they weren't so far apart. When he conversed with his new brothers, he wanted to gaze into their eyes. It didn't matter now, but he wanted them to know that what the racist cops said about him were lies. "As you know, I'm also home early from a place named Staten Island, New York." Surprisingly at this time, Eric felt nervous so he picked up a brussel sprout with his fork. Continuing his introduction while politely chewing, Eric said he was forty three years old. He added that when he was traveling home too soon, his story was still being told. His murder made the world news but he wished that wasn't how it went. Although he felt safe in the University, he was extremely angry at how he was sent. Still chewing the brussel sprout, Eric was afraid that again he would choke. Remembering that feeling, he grinded down the small vegetable before he even spoke. As an extra precautionary measure, Eric picked up his diamond cut glass to drink. The cold water on his tongue and in the back of his throat cleared his mind so he could think. With his mouth and lips clear of any food, he wiped them with his satin napkin just because. He cleared his throat and said to his brothers, Okay, this is how it was. I was in my own neighborhood just chillin' while I was walking. All of a sudden I heard a radio with people on it talking. When I looked behind me I saw some cops, of course they all were white. Before I could even turn back around, one accosted me on a whim. I had no idea why he was doing this to me when I knew I did nothing to him. When he first tried to put his hands on me, I instinctively pushed one away. Racist cops always harassed me and I told them that I was tired of it that day. The first officer tried to throw me to the ground, but he couldn't 'cause he was a lightweight. So his racist partners joined him in beating me; my body and heart feeling all of their hate. While I was being attacked I kept yelling 'get off of me, get off of me'". But still they wouldn't let me be. Seeing as though that plea was of no use, I started yelling 'I ain't do nothing, 'I ain't do nothing; what did I do'"? They wrongfully told me that I was resisting arrest and selling Loosies too". "What are Loosies"? Trayvon asked; "what are Loosies, big brothers?". George chimed in and replied, "it's one cigarette from a pack without all the rest". Tray nodded his head to express his newly found understanding. But as he did he suddenly felt some tension in his chest. Secretly, he didn't want to hear anymore because it made him too upset. But at the same time he quietly prayed that a judge's thrown book, the racist cops would get. Trayvon noticed that throughout Eric's speaking, Amadou had no questions nor statements to make. But Amadou knew what Tray was feeling, and wanted Eric to stop for his little brother's sake. But Eric had no clue as to what Tray was feeling, no one told him the deal. He didn't know there needed to be a break in his story in order to give Tray's heart time to heal. So, Eric continued educating his little brothers about all the punches racist cops made him feel. As if to save the worst for less, Eric said, "Now listen to this part". Then he began telling them about the ending as if it was the start. He began again: "All of those racists were able to throw me to the ground and tackle me, so there was nothing I could do. In his head, Trayvon said to Eric, "Big brother, I feel sorry for you". "Now this is where the worst part comes into play", Eric said. And before he continued, he took another deep breath as he also shook his head. He began again: "Once I was on the ground, all the cops were holding my body down. I remember thinking, 'Each pig's face is probably wearing a smile while mine alone a frown'. One of the pigs held my neck with his arm so that it couldn't move. My hands were already cuffed behind my back, so what did they really have to prove? The racist cop held my neck so tight that I felt as if I was choking. Eleven times I yelled, 'I can't breathe', but he continued as if I was joking. I already had asthma so this chokehold just made things worse. Before I knew it I couldn't speak, even though I wanted to curse. Before my inability to speak started, the witnesses had formed a crowd. While losing my breath I hoped they'd report that my eleven screams of 'I can't breathe' were very loud. The next thing I remember, I was floating in the sky. With my eyes closed and my body feeling light, I was unafraid and I didn't know why. I remember floating on one level of the clouds but then I moved higher to another. Then my hand joined someone else's; I recognized it as the hand of my brother. Hand in Hand we slowly floated downward and I was afraid I'd painfully hit the ground. But when I reached the bottom of the cloud, there was no ground to even be found. Instead I landed gracefully with pillows of clouds beneath my feet. Some pain still on my body and quite a bit on my neck, I remembered that I'd been beat. George and I looked at each other as if we'd never met. We stared into each other's eyes and knew it wasn't time for us to return yet. Neither of us could speak and each of our necks were sore. It was a pain that I couldn't even remember ever feeling before. George and I had to speak with our eyes which agreed we'd stay together. We didn't know if that would mean until the end of that experience or until the time of forever. With our hands remaining clasped, we looked ahead and before us to see the brightest of the brightest light. As we walked toward it, I knew it could never be put out by the night. As we walked, we exercised our necks. We saw before us beautiful mansions with many levels or decks. At once my feet no longer touched pillows of clouds, instead they felt a little cold. I looked down to see why this was so and found them standing on a street of gold. George and I looked at each other and our eyes told us we were home. And towards the East I saw what I remembered to be the University Dome. With our eyes meeting once again, George and I picked up our pace. We lived for the time when once again we'd see The Master's face. When we reached the pearly gate, in awe I could say nothing at all. Nothing around me appeared tiny or small; all the beautiful mansions were tall. Once the gate opened and I saw the man I very first knew, my mouth opened widely, and I just didn't know what to do. I noticed that in a whisper I was now able to speak words. I looked upward from whence we'd come and I now noticed beautiful birds. Speaking my words started out very slow, but then they moved faster and faster. There were only three words I wanted to say and they were, 'That's The Master'. While I dropped to my knees, I was able to speak those words while on his knees, George twice yelled 'Momma'. I didn't know why, but it sounded as though he was reliving some sort of trauma. Looking up into His face from my knees, all I could do was cry. 'Is that you Master?', I cautiously asked. "Yes my son; it is I'".

END OF CHAPTER 8

Was It Fake Or Were They Mistaken?

(Who Cares? His Life Should Not Have Been Taken)

At the end of Eric's introduction to his brothers, the three of them turned to George to now speak. The room went silent as it appeared to them that George's words he tried to seek. "I, I, I" he started, and he couldn't get out the rest. A tear landed on George's buttered roll while at the same time he clinched his chest. Amadou and Trayvon wondered what exactly this meant and they hoped that George was well. Eric immediately comforted him, "He's okay but his introduction may be hard to tell". Patiently waiting, the brothers watched each other with eyes agreeing to give George some time. Eric perceived that his brother had it rough as soon as he heard the welcome chime. Slowly releasing his hands from his chest, he used his satin napkin to dry his eyes. Eric felt George was ready to talk but he told himself, "Remain patient until he tries". With eyes now dry and his chest hands-free, George tried to begin again. He still felt the trauma fighting him inside, but he told himself, "I will win". He tried to begin again: "I, I, I, I'm sorry my brothers; I had to get myself together in order to give my introduction. Sometimes I have flashes going on in my head and it makes it hard for my words to function". Eric responded, "It's alright George, don't worry about it, you know you'll be okay". George cleared his throat in a nervous jester responding, "Okay, this is what I wanted to say. First of all Eric, I cannot believe how our earthly lives were the same. Your introduction could've been mine if only you had changed your name. I thought no one on earth could have my story. I thought, 'There's no one who knows'". Anyway, I guess I should go on ahead and tell you guys how my introduction goes". George focused his eyes on Amadou and Trayvon as he began again: "Well, as you now know, my name is George Floyd and I'm your bigger big brother. Eric and I were introduced by family on earth and we each had our own mother. Just like Eric I used cigarettes, so we were both smokers. Another thing we had in common was racist cops treating us like jokers. I worked at a burger joint, but when I lost that job I worked security at a bar. I was struggling to make ends meet, but I was able to hold onto my car. I drove to a Mom and Pop Shop to buy a pack of cigs; no big thang 'cause I did that a lot. I remember I was wearing my Wife Beater 'cause on that day it was hot. All I wanted to do was go in and out, you know, get what I came to get. I said, "what's up" to the dudes; even gave one a pound 'cause we'd already met. He asked me if I wanted my usual, I put my twenty on the counter and said, "You know it". I started opening the pack as soon as they were in my hands, I couldn't wait to inhale and blow it. Dude turned towards the register and complemented the day while I stood there waitin' on my change. For some reason I don't even remember how much the cigs cost; maybe somewhere in the six dollar range. Anyway, I grabbed my change, stuck it in my pocket, and I was on my way. 'Peace out', I said to my man, because that's what I'd always say. By the time I got outside the store my lips already held the lit cig. Feeling thankful that I even had the twenty to buy them, inside I felt kinda big. My truck was already parked in front of the store so I jumped in as I took a puff, and I calmly shut my door. Before I knew it two Youngins out of nowhere started banging on my glass. My window was up but I thought I heard the word "fake", and those Youngins must've thought they could whip my ass. I let my window down, they tried to snatch my smokes, and I didn't know what else they wanted to do. I asked them what was goin' on, and they said my twenty wasn't real. I looked at them boys like they was crazy and I said, 'Look now, I don't steal'". They ain't never heard me yell before, that's why I think they jumped back. Outta nowhere I heard sirens and felt cops pulling on me as I said, 'Give me some slack'". They forcefully grabbed me from my truck and made me put my Cig out. They also said my bill was fake but I told him it was real without a doubt. The more I tried to convince them, the tighter they held my wife beater. Before I knew it they ripped it off and that's when I started to feel the pain. So many blacks were killed by racist cops so I thought this was insane. Real quick I wondered how and why they got there; I was like, "Who even called the Popo"? The Youngins were egging them on while I was trying to tell them about my dough. 'There's no way I would pass a fake bill', I said, 'that's not how I was raised'. Those racist cops threw me against my truck which met my eye, and right then my vision was glazed. They started beating me so bad y'all, I saw blood running down my chest. I didn't even know where it came from; maybe my head or mouth at best. The racist cops grabbed my wrists and pulled them into my back. Right after that, my wrists felt cold and I'll never forget that sound, 'click clack'. I assumed that meant that I was under arrest but still they didn't tell me what I did. I kept telling them that my twenty wasn't fake, so I shouldn't have to do that bid. A couple of the cops told me to stay outside of my truck while others were telling me to get back in. I thought to myself, 'these pigs don't know what they want me to do', but in the end I knew they would win. More police cars came and surrounded my truck even though I couldn't go nowhere. People started comin' aroun' to see what was goin' on. I looked to my left and my good eye was right; my dude from the store was there. He looked as if he felt sorry for me and I couldn't understand that. I wanted to yell to him, 'show 'em my bill, tell 'em it's real, come on my man you can't do that'? Naked from the waist up with old and new blood on my chest, the racist cops put me in their car. I ain't know where they were takin' me, but I hoped it wasn't far. Still bloody and cuffed with that glaze in my one eye, the racist cops dragged me out of their car. At this point I was hurtin' so bad I knew I'd be left with more than just a scar. I still don't know why, but the racist cops pulled me out of their car, threw me on the ground, and shackled my feet. I wondered how I could end up on the ground when minutes before I was sitting in my own car's seat. It felt like those pigs wanted to beat me to a pulp, and once again I felt that blood flow. Even if they didn't see it, I know they heard me say, 'Let me go'. Before I knew it I was laying on my stomach, cuffed and shackled with my face held to the ground. Just like you Eric, I vividly remember a crowd of people coming around. Because of the position they put me in, I couldn't move my face and my head could only lay on the left. Now remember I said my eye met my truck? Well, that was the eye on that same side. My right eye worked better, but I was thrown to the ground, so even the vision from that one was hazy. Through that eye I saw four white cops, one was handling me aggressively. I wondered why the other ones stood, watched, and did nothing. After all, I was just one person but together they made three. I thought I was gonna lose my voice because I was screaming so loud. My entire body was hurting from the assault so that was not the time to be proud. The way that racist cop beat me, I thought my entire body was a wreck. I never would have imagined feelin' his knee on my neck. Believe that shit? I could go nowhere but he felt my neck should be pinned. Now remember, I did absolutely nothing, yet they beat me as if I'd badly sinned. Anyway, I felt more blood flowing, but this time I knew it was from my nose. I couldn't even wipe it because remember, I was cuffed. At this point I knew my internal blood rose. I started to doubt myself; 'maybe my twenty was fake'. But even if so, I swear I didn't know, so that assault I shouldn't have been forced to take. The racist cop put more and more pressure on my neck whenever he wanted to. He ignored my screams, pleads, and question; 'Officer, what did I do'? One of the other three pigs told me to stand up as if my body was free. I yelled, 'I can't, I can't, I can't get up; my neck is pinned by his knee'. I yelled so loud, 'my neck hurts, my stomach hurts, everything hurts; please don't kill me, please'. Comfortably, the punk kept his knee on my neck as the hot ground held up my knees. When the knee punk pinned my neck tighter, I screamed and one of the others mimicked me. How in hell could he do that when he saw what was happening?; he was right there; he could see. I remember being very thirsty and I yelled out, 'water, water'. When they ignored my request, I thought I'd pass out and I remember thinking about my daughter. Of course I wanted to stay alive for myself but I definitely wanted to stay for her. I tried to keep her beautiful face in my thoughts but it was hard 'cause it started to blur. The crowd sounded large and it sounded like they were rooting for me. But my glazed eye saw that they were being kept back from the remaining pigs of three. Faintly I heard them pleading for me that I couldn't breathe, there was no way. One of the racist cops responded, 'He's talking, so he's okay'. When I started feeling as if my life was slipping, I yelled for my Momma who seemed to be near. There was no shadow of doubt in my mind that my pleas for her help, my Momma did hear. I remembered feeling a new and bubbly flow coming from my mouth's corner on the right. The pressure on my neck was getting tighter and tighter and I had no more will to fight. The last thing I remember is floating in the sky on each and each cloud. Unlike the crowd that watched my suffering, this trip was pleasant and not loud. I was surprised to meet Eric up there, but both of us seemed to be fine. His eyes spoke love and care for me, so he put his hand in mine. We landed together, followed the light, and The Master met us at the gate's door. I immediately knew that I'd returned to the University and pain would be no more. I dropped to my knees because I knew that I was really free. But I also dropped to them because I knew my Momma I was gonna see. The Master said He had to prepare her to see me here first". At this point George picked up his diamond glass because he had to quench his thirst. "So, that's who I am and how I returned. I'm glad I got that out; wow!" In anticipation, George rubbed his knees and said, "I'm waiting for my Momma now".

END OF CHAPTER 9

Screaming For Her After the Chase

(But Now I See Her Face)

Excitedly George turned towards the dining room's door and could not contain his emotions. He looked at The Master inquisitively thinking "He must have made some potions". His eyes now clear, he viewed the woman holding hands with The Master. George stood up to slowly walk to her. But without his control, his feet on their own, they caused him to walk faster. He knew the dining room was long, but at this time it seemed to be even longer. As he pushed on with tears streaming down his face, he felt his legs getting stronger. Then in front of the woman, George paused to be certain who she was. And then he heard The Master's introduction as he and his brothers always does. Just as his hand was with Eric's when from above, they were floating down, The Master put George's hand into the woman's who George noticed was wearing a beautiful crown. "George my son", The Master began, "I trust the introductions amongst your brothers were nice. And now I want to re-introduce you to your Momma; the one you yelled for twice".

END OF CHAPTER 10

The Brothers Start To Get Down

(With Their D.J. Michael Brown)

George and his Momma held each other's hands as if they'd never let them go. It mattered not to either of them that they allowed their tears of joy to show. Hands now released, the both of them stopped somewhere in the middle of the long hall. Momma looked her son over, rubbed his face, kissed him on his lips, and told him he'd grown so tall. Meanwhile, the other three brothers looked at one another with smiles that spoke their words. And just for a moment the three of them recognized the lovely sound of the birds. They agreed that it was better to hear the songs from the birds as opposed to the sound from the welcome chimes. They knew that sound meant another brother coming home too soon; forced to say good-bye to former times. George turned his head back to his brothers to let them know he'd see them later. The six eyes watched as they waved their hands knowing that this re-introduction would be greater. They watched their brother continue to walk with his Momma until they could no longer be seen. With eyes so keen, Amadou looked at Trayvon, bumped his shoulder and went in for the lean. "What's up, Little Brother"?, Amadou asked. You got something you wanna say"? Trayvon shyly whispered in his ear, "Let's teach him the game we played earlier today". "Okay little brother, you don't have to be shy, Eric's your Big Brother too". "What's up Little Man? " Eric asked; "Is there something you wanna do"? Trayvon answered, "Amadou taught me a really fun game and I want you to learn it too". "Ain't no thang then, let's get started, I'mma beat you both anyway". Amadou had been given the University tour by The Master when he first came. He needed to show Eric his own mansion before they'd teach him the game. In awe Eric opened the door which he couldn't believe was his favorite color of blue. The Master knew all about him, but he was surprised that He knew that too. The three brothers toured Eric's mansion which took at least two hours. He didn't care for their scent while he was on earth, but during this tour, he loved the smell of his flowers. Trayvon told his Big Brothers that Eric's mansion looked a lot like his. Amadou agreed and said to his brothers, "Follow me; I'll show you guys where mine is". While following, Trayvon softly asked Amadou if he could show Eric his mansion too. Amadou reminded him that everyday was everyday and he could do whatever he wanted to do. Trayvon looked up at Eric, found his eyes, and said, "You'll see my mansion after Amadou's". He told his Big Brother he had all kinds of sneakers which The Master sometimes called "shoes". Arriving at Amadou's mansion, Eric noticed that his door was made of beautiful jade. He complimented Amadou who said, "The

Master knew me well, so this is what He made". The Brothers toured Amadou's mansion for about ninety minutes or so. As with Eric's, they didn't tour the entire mansion, but they'd planned to continue later though. Amadou wanted Eric to see Trayvon's mansion before they taught him the game. As soon as they arrived, he immediately saw that the colorful door held Trayvon's name. Tray explained to Eric why his multicolored door was grand. "The Master knew I loved skittles, and they were the last thing I held in my hand". He further explained that he'd never again be without them 'cause The Master included them in his handmade Candyland. Because it was definitely his favorite, this room was the first that Trayvon introduced. Feeling a bit tired after his big meal, he popped some skittles in his mouth for an energy boost. He told his brothers that if they ever got a sweet tooth, they could always stop by and choose from his Candyland. He told them that The Master provided customized bags so they didn't have to hold any in their hand. Trayvon's older brothers thanked him as they noticed the candy in the room shine. And just then, Trayvon let them know, "I'll share with you everything that's mine". His older brothers thanked him and promised that they'd do the same. The tour inside Tray's mansion wasn't as long as the others because they were all interested in the game. All of them knew that they could always return and listen to whatever Tray may have to say. After all, they were getting used to every day being every day. Suddenly, Eric stopped in his tracks to say that each of them forgot to lock his door. But Amadou informed him that the University was safe; break-ins and robberies were no more. Trayvon then thought to himself, "So that's how The Master got in. He unlocked my door in order to prove that the University held no robbers within". Amadou led his brothers to the Great Rooms which The Master gave no names. He decided that everyday to everyday, that's where he'd teach and play his games. Trayvon and Eric entered one and agreed that the room was in fact "GREAT"! With another Alexa and a karaoke machine, they'd have a lot of fun, and they could hardly wait. Sitting in plush recliners at one of the marble tables, Amadou began: "Okay Eric, let's get this started. Now this is how the game will go". Suddenly Trayvon happily interrupted , "Wait Big Brother, let me teach him; I remember how, I know". "You sure you got this, Little Brother? You sure you can tell Eric what to do"? "I'm remembering better in the University" he said, "and if I need help I know you'll be here too. "Sho ya' right Little Brother. You're learning how we'll live in the University now. You're catching on quick, Little Guy. Pretty soon YOU'LL be teaching ME how". Trayvon explained the rules of the game to Eric, and Amadou found them to be correct. In fact, Trayvon explained them so well that there was no need for Amadou to interject. Eric confirmed that he understood and knew what he'd have to do to play. Because he'd already introduced himself to his brothers and they now knew much more than his name, he asked his Little Brothers if it would be okay if he'd play the game a different way. He told them when he listened to music on Earth, he liked to listen to a guy named Michael Brown. He was a musician who loved his Beats and when he performed, he really got down. "When I was on Earth, Michael taught me how to rap and if I say so myself, I'm pretty good". Trayvon asked him if he could hear him perform and Eric said he soon would. He began telling them how he met Michael Brown,

Jr. when he performed at a small joint. He told them that "Big Mike" was off the chain, and definitely didn't disappoint. "Not very long after Michael Jackson died I met up with "Big Mike" again one afternoon. He said he was planning a block party for The King of Pop real soon. He said he had an assignment for me which would prove if I'd learned how to rap. I wasn't confident about staying on beat, so I knew I'd have to work on my hand clap. Not knowing what my assignment would be, I practiced "Big Mike's lessons everyday. If I had to prove that I knew how to rap, I knew I had to have rhyming words to say. A few weeks later I was surprised when "Big Mike" hit me up on my cell. When I saw his name on the screen, I couldn't front, I was nervous as hell. But I took the call like a champ and said, 'What's up, Big Mike? What's going on'"? You got that assignment for me yet"? He said, 'Sho 'ya right, Big E; I'mma give it to you now so when the time comes you'll be set'. "'Aight, I'm listening, my man", I said with elation. Big Mike reminded me about the block party and said he needed an invitation. I was taken aback but I continued to listen so that not one word I'd miss. He said, 'I want you to create the invitation to the block party, but the way I want it is like this. I want the date, the location, and the time when it will go down. I'll have something there for the children; maybe some games or even a clown. I've never given out an invitation like this, and you know I do parties all the time. But here's the thang though, E, here's the thang. I want you to create it as if it's a rap and I want the entire invitation to rhyme'. I knew I'd have no problem with a simple invitation, but the other orders seemed real tall. I knew somehow I had to make it work; I couldn't make "Big Mike" look small. I told Michael that I had him and asked how much time I'd be given. He responded, 'Wait, there's one more thing; This original invitation must include songs that The King of Pop made when he was livin'. I was glad that Michael couldn't see my eyes popping out of my head. I loved Michael Jackson and was sad when he died, but now I REALLY wished he wasn't dead.! I immediately wanted to give it up and tell "Big Mike" I couldn't do this. But I remained on the phone, shut my eyes, and gathered my thoughts in my head. I again asked Michael how much time I had and Michael gave me weeks of two. He attempted to encourage me as he said, 'Come on "E", you got this; just show me what I've been teaching you'". Eric told Amadou and Trayvon that he was scared as hell because he didn't want to let "Big Mike" down. He thought if he did, Michael would gather together the children at the party and make HIM the laughing clown. Finally, he told his brothers that the invitation was his toughest assignment ever. But he came through for "Big Mike", and yes, the entire invitation did rhyme. He also threw in the Michael Jackson songs and everything was done in time. Having the two weeks which "Big Mike" gave Eric to complete his assignment, he needed to use them all. But he was just glad that he came through for him and that he answered the call. Back in the Great Room he rubbed his hands together then slid them from his nose to his chin. And he prepared himself to spit for his brothers the way he spat for the neighborhood back then. Eric said he had to tell the neighborhood that they'd been invited to the block party which would be happening that next week. With courage in his heart and sweat on his brow, he used a megaphone to speak. In the Great Room, Eric couldn't tell who was most excited to hear his talent;

Trayvon or Amadou. So before he began he said to them, "Here it go; I'll spit it for the both of you". And he began:

END OF CHAPTER 11

From The Bottom, But to The Top

(For Michael Jackson, "The King Of Pop")

"You are cordially invited to ENJOY YOURSELF. There's going to be a block party to remember MICHAEL JACKSON a.k.a. M.J. You're getting this invitation so I can ROCK WITH YOU, September 7th is the day. Of course I'LL BE THERE; I'm THE LIFE OF THE PARTY, I'm always on the scene. We'll COME TOGETHER whether we're BLACK OR WHITE to create one big DANCING MACHINE. There will be games for the kids, prizes for best performance, best look alike, and best dressed. "Big Mike" will be spinning MICHAEL JACKSON all day, so bring your SMILE, come and be blessed. The party starts at "1" with kids dancing to THRILLER. So come, order a smoothie, and be seated. M.J. said, "DON'T STOP 'TIL YOU GET ENOUGH", so we'll party 'til the cops say 'BEAT IT'! Feel free to bring a friend so YOU ARE NOT ALONE: BEN, LITTLE SUSIE, BILLY JEAN; bring 'em all. MAYBE TOMORROW you'll tell me you'll come 'cause this party will be OFF THE WALL. AT 1 MLK, JR. Street is where we'll reminisce about what we as a people had. We'll REMEMBER THE TIME M.J. gave us the Moon Walk, and the time he let us know that he was BAD. Everyone is welcome; your little boy or girl. You can bring your SUGAR DADDY, ROCKIN' ROBIN or MAMA'S PEARL. You need to be at this party; not LOOKIN' THROUGH THE WINDOWS; you need to share memories of your own. We NEVER CAN SAY GOODBYE to MICHAEL JACKSON; The Greatest King of Pop; it's true. But on September 7th we'll SCREAM to M.J., 'I JUST CAN'T STOP LOVING YOU'. Michael wanted to HEAL THE WORLD; the greatest desire of his heart. So come to this block party and we can show M.J. that we're doing it; We're making a start." "Just like that", Eric said to his brothers, "That was my shout. And at the end I lowered my megaphone and said, 'I'm 'Eric and I'm out'"! Eric's brothers were talking to him about wanting to hear another rhyme. Since everyday was everyday, they knew they'd have the time. Suddenly they stopped and turned towards the door 'cause they heard the familiar welcome chime. Amadou, Trayvon and Eric decided to greet whomever was at the gate. Although their fast paces turned into jogs, they found that they were too late. The Master was walking towards them with yet another young man for them to meet. Amadou thought, "Whomever he is, I'll offer him a seat". When the Master and the young man approached the brothers, Eric dropped to his knees, face down. Then they heard The Master say to them, "My sons, meet your brother, Michael Brown.

END OF CHAPTER 12

I Thought I Knew You Then

(Eric Meets "Big Mike" Again)

The brothers were speechless as they thought of Eric's invitation, the block party, and the clown. Looking at their brother then back up to the Master, each of them wondered, "Could he be THEE Michael Brown?". Rising from his knees with tears streaming down his face, Eric tightly held the young man. "Big Mike", he cried. "Yo, it's good to see you again, my man. Looka here, my man; lemme introduce you to the clan. We were just talkin' 'bout you. I was telling them what a great musician and rapper you were when we were buddies down on Earth. Bruh, we were so tight down there that I thought we knew each other since birth. I see you still rockin' ya' headphones the way you did back in the day. Don't worry, Little brothers, they're not on, he can hear everything we say". Just then, Big Mike removed his Beats Headphones from his ears and transferred them to his neck. He didn't fully believe that he was no longer on Earth, so he walked around a little just to check.

"Master?", he said, "You told me I was back at the University. But why? I was only eighteen". "I can answer that myself", Eric said; " We're all here 'cause the racist whites were mean". Eric introduced his newly arrived brother to Amadou and Trayvon as they remained in the hall. The Master stepped back and said to Big Mike, "These are your brothers and I love you all. On Earth you were loved by your family, friends, and all the rest. But here at the University, you will find that I, The Master, love you best". The brothers watched as He turned and walked away, but not in the direction from whence He came. Unknowingly, each of the brothers thought the same: "Another brother has come home too soon to play the Name Game. Amadou's eyes scanned those of Big Mike's and quickly those of the other two. Speaking to the three of them, Amadou said, "Follow me, there's something we need to do". Eric and Trayvon again walked on each side of Amadou as big Mike fell just a little bit behind. This was due to the taking in of his surroundings and realizing the University was one-of-a-kind. Picking up his pace, as he walked, he admired every ceiling light. He finally caught up when he heard Eric say to Amadou, "Hold up, something ain't right. I remember the Great Room being around the corner and immediately to the left. We're going straight; what's up with that"? "We were in the Great Room", Amadou answered. I know where that's at. I want us to hang out in the Greater Room; it's a five minute walk to it's amethyst door". Whispering to himself, Big Mike said, "Now I KNOW I'm not in Missouri anymore". Arriving at the amethyst door, Amadou held his hand over a diamond square. Immediately the humongous doors opened inward and the other brothers could only stare. "WOWWWW" was what all three of the brothers could say. Quiet Amadou wasn't surprised, he understood everyday being everyday. Eric noticed that Amadou's face was blank and that he never even cracked a smile. "What's going on little brother"? he asked Amadou. "You don't like the style? You never seem phased by anything in the University even though it's brand new". "Everyday is everyday so these things I can always see and do. Not everyone who returns to the University would remember that these things are old; not new". The brothers didn't understand anything Amadou was saying. Trayvon didn't even try; his mind was strictly on the Name Game playing. "Aye Bruh", Eric said to Amadou. "How do you know your way around the University? Have you been here before?". "I was an infant but when I returned The Master gave me a tour. Big Mike asked, "How long did it take you to finally know your way"? "I wish I could answer that for you Big Mike, but I can't because everyday is everyday". Big Mike looked at his brother wanting to ask, "Amadou what do you mean?". Instead, he held back his tongue and continued to be in awe at what he'd seen. Inside The Greater Room Amadou led his brothers to an already opened coral gate. Trayvon was the first to run inside as if he didn't want to be late. "Woh, woh, 'Tray', slow down", Amadou said. You ain't gotta rush like that. Remember what I told you, "everyday is everyday, so everything will stay where it's at". Eric told Trayvon that he could be the one to pick out the game table. Though happy to have received the assignment, there were so many so he hoped he'd be able. Running around the room from one side to another, Trayvon didn't know which to choose. "Come on Little Bruh", Eric said. "Either one you pick is cool 'cause we can't lose". Slowing down but out of breath Trayvon knew he needed a break. Bent over with his hands on his knees, he looked left to see a window, and through it, a lake. "OMG", he said, as he seemed hypnotized by how the water flowed. He didn't mind that the name game would be delayed due to his "table assignment" being slowed. Amadou approached his brother and placed his hand on his spine. "You're okay, Little Brother. You don't have to stay here wondering how the water flows that way. You can look at it whenever you want 'cause'". Trayvon proudly finished his brother's sentence: "Everyday is everyday". As Trayvon stood up straight, he turned to see Eric and said, "I'm sorry Big Brother, I had to catch my breath 'cause I was tired". Eric chuckled, "Aight Little Brother, choose the table now, 'cause you were 'bout to be fired". Trayvon chose a table closest to another entry door.

END OF CHAPTER 13

Music In the Air

(Until The Brothers Meet Another Pair)

The four brothers sat at the table finally chosen by the youngest of the clan. Eric looked at Trayvon with a smile and said, You aight little man. Amadou explained to his brothers that he chose The Greater Room because of the DJ equipment it had. He knew that added feature would definitely satisfy Big Mike; he knew it would make him glad. Big Mike inquisitively approached the equipment which was somewhat like the one he had. He was extremely happy to see his name on the equipment and now he'd be his brothers' comrade. Big Mike quickly found the power button and pushed it so he could start. He was very happy to once again do what was always in his heart. Removing the left side of his Beats from his neck, he put the earpiece to his ear. The way in which he worked his profession, he only needed one from which to hear. Vinyls with various artists' names were in Big Mike's D.J. Booth made of glass and gold. On Earth he never owned most of them, they were the ones with millions of copies sold. Big Mike's brothers encouraged him to work the turntables and scratch the records to show them what he could do. "Aight, aight, ready? I'mma spit a little something for you". Minutes after Big Mike began, his flow was quickly interrupted and the music stopped on a dime. The brothers heard what by now they'd gotten used to: The sound of the welcome chime. Big Mike left his booth and joined his brothers as they discussed if they should make the greeting at the gate. They decided that wouldn't work because the walk was too long so they'd surely be too late. "At the very least", Eric said, "We can sit at a table near the first entrance and wait". The other three brothers agreed and Trayvon said, "Big Brother, that idea is great". Jogging towards the entrance to the beautiful coral gate, Trayvon immediately chose the table and the four of them sat. After conversing amongst each other their facial expressions went flat. They wondered who would be arriving next; who would sit where they sat? Not very long after, the brothers heard slight whispers in the air. They looked towards the coral door and thought they saw three people there. After shaking their heads to clear their eyes, aside from the Master, there was a pair. Trayvon noticed that the younger was a boy who looked even younger than he. Big Mike was the most recent to arrive so neither did he know to be. Amadou, Trayvon, and Eric recognized the brother they'd met sometime before. So they only had one man to meet, but of course Big Mike had more. When the Master arrived at the table with the two, the four stood but they didn't know why they did. The young boy appeared to be shy as behind the Master and George he hid. When the Master and George placed the boy between them, the brothers discovered that he was just a kid. Now clinging to George's side, the child continued to look down. Eric thought back to his block party invitation and knew that the child could have played with the clown. The Master once again broke the silence which the brothers had between each other. "My sons, I too am vexed with these introductions, but I must have you meet another. Michael, this is your big brother George whom your brothers have already met. And this little boy here is extremely shy and aside from me it's only George he's met. Take him under your wings, show him around, and love him; he's very shy, but nice. My sons please meet your youngest brother; his name is Tamir Rice.

END OF CHAPTER 14

Annoyed Or Overjoyed?

(He Remembers The Story Of George Floyd)

Trayvon was the first to approach Tamir and he did so as slowly as he could. He remembered the way Amadou hugged him when he arrived so he thought that he really should. With his head still down but now in his big brother's embrace, Tamir loved that Trayvon held him tight. Being taken from his earthly family felt wrong, but for some reason this felt right. The older brothers watched this connection a while before they came to join in too. Without even thinking about it, this is what they wanted to do. They walked him back to the very large table where they had been sitting. Amadou thought a formal introduction for Tamir would definitely be fitting. Trayvon whispered to his older brother, "I think he's too young to play the name game but I can teach him a different way. We could just let him tell us all about himself but his words don't have to rhyme. Besides, Big Mike is here now and he can teach him in due time". "That's a great idea, Trayvon", his big brother Eric said. "The important thing is that we get to know him; it's okay if he just talks plainly instead". Trayvon said to Tamir, "It's okay if you're a little shy; I was that way when I first came too. Our brother Amadou knows this place well and he'll teach you where to go and what to do". Amadou asked George how he ended up being with Tamir and the Master when they thought he was visiting with his Momma. He said he got lost after the visitation and ended up at the Safe Safari petting a llama. He then started to walk towards the wrong way again, but The Master found him in time. As He was escorting him back to the Great Room, they heard the welcome chime. So that he wouldn't get lost again, he went to the gate with the Master. He noticed when the welcome chime rang, the Master moved faster on His feet. It was hard for George to keep up, but he tried because he wanted to see who he'd meet. When the Master opened the gate, Tamir stood in front of it crying. George couldn't wait to welcome him and teach him why they'll be no more dying. The Master hugged Tamir tightly and told him he was home too soon. On Earth he was aware how time passes because there was a sun and a moon. The Master held his hand out to Tamir; he'd take it and slowly walk. George explained to his brothers that the walk to the Great Room was quiet because Tamir couldn't seem to talk. He asked his brothers how they ended up in the room which was now greater. Amadou responded, "Let's get on with the game, we'll explain all that later". George noticed that while he was speaking to his brothers, Big Mike never looked away. It seemed to George that he must've had something he wanted to say. Excluding Big Mike, the brothers started to walk towards where the equipment was stored. Especially George, but all the brothers wondered why Big Mike suddenly looked bored. George stopped, looked back at Big Mike and asked, "Aren't you coming with us Bro? Remember, we're alive, not dead". Big Mike responded, "I never knew you were my brother, but George I think I know you". "Don't forget, we both came from earth, Big Mike, so there's a possibility that you do". He noticed the indentation on the back of George's neck which looked like the top of a knee. George saw big Mike staring at his neck so he grabbed it and said, "I bet you do know me". "Yes", Big Mike said "And now I know how I do. The entire world down on Earth watched what happened to you. You are the man who twice screamed for his Momma when your neck you could not relieve. You are the man who was also cuffed and shackled while at least sixteen times yelling, "I can't breathe". George responded, "Yea, that's me, but the pain is all behind me now. The only thing that's left in my heart is the question to my murderer: 'How'"? Big Mike gave his new big brother a pound, and a hug tighter than any others. And so began this loving relationship with the two similar brothers. Both of them jogged down the hall to catch up with the others. When the brothers in the front heard George and Big Mike coming, they kept their feet on the ground to wait. Amadou looked at all of his brothers and thought, "I'm glad they were at the gate".

END OF CHAPTER 15

After He Remembers That Time

❦

("Big Mike" Spits Floyd's Story In A Rhyme)

As the four brothers walked together towards the Great Room, the tall ceiling lights seemed to shine a bit brighter. And although he didn't know it, Tamir's burden was even lighter. The brothers showed him around the Great before showing him around the Greater Room. Tamir's eyes lit up like the New York City Christmas Tree which he remembered seeing before. And little by little he told himself, "I'm not really homesick anymore". Having been given the Great Room Tour, his older brothers were ready to go. Tamir appeared as though he didn't want to leave; this was true because he told them so. Trayvon gently placed his hand on his little brother's shoulder saying, "We have a room even greater". He loosely took Tamir's hand, slowly walked him towards the door, and assured him, "You can always come back later". Tamir seemed to gain trust in Trayvon so he placed a tighter grip on his hand. Now walking closely as brothers should, Trayvon told him all about his Candyland. As the older brothers moved towards the Greater Room, the younger two lagged behind while talking. Thinking this was cool, the older brothers shared more information about each other as they did their own walking. Soon to arrive at the Greater Room, the two youngest brothers now ran ahead. Amadou wanted to give Tamir the tour, Trayvon wanted to do it instead. Trayvon remembered how heavy the door was, but wanted to open it alone if he could. When he was unable, he asked Tamir to give him a hand if he would. The elders knew Trayvon wanted to try things on his own, so there they watched, and there they stood. To their surprise the youngsters were able to open the door while their elders stood at the entrance in awe. Never would they have believed that the boys were that strong, they couldn't believe what they saw. He needed some help with the tour from Amadou but overall Trayvon did well. The brothers knew he was proud of himself; with the Kool-Aid smile glued to his face, it was easy for them to tell. Tamir was again in awe of the Greater Room and when he saw Big Mike's equipment, he was amazed. Stopping at the DJ booth, he touched the glass door, and instantly his eyes were glazed. He looked at Trayvon with those eyes and quietly asked, "Who does all of this belong to"? Just then, Big Mike answered, "It's mine. Come on little man, let me show it to you". Tamir looked at big Mike bewilderedly and responded, "Huh? You'll really do that"? Big Mike escorted Tamir into the booth and showed him where all the gadgets were at. In a brief lesson to his brother, the others heard, "See Tamir? You do it like that". Big Mike explained to Tamir that he had something he needed to do; he hoped he wouldn't be annoyed. He stuck his head out of the doorway of the booth to say, "This one's for you, my brother George Floyd". George was the first to turn towards the voice of Big Mike's and then the others did too. George immediately asked his brother what he was about to do. He explained to George that when he watched him being murdered it was just too much to take. He put his anger into his music and knew there was a rap he had to make. While writing the rap, tears streamed down his face, but Big Mike knew he had to push through. He wanted to get revenge for what the Blues did, but he knew that wasn't the right thing to do. Every television station tuned in as all of George's pleas were heard. With his face soaked and pen and paper at hand, with every plea Mike found a word. As he wrote this piece for his unknown brother, his anger slowly started to dissipate. He realized that with his words and music, he could conquer hate. So Big Mike explained this to his brothers and at the end a tear fell from his eye. He admitted not knowing if he'd get through his rap, but assured them that he would try. He closed the glass door with the diamond handle and he entered his very own booth. He checked his mic, put his Beats Headphones over both his ears, and begin to speak the truth:

"And Yet Another Black Man Couldn't Breathe"

"The other officers stood silent, nope they never made a sound. Instead they watched their partner kill George Floyd while he was on the ground. They did absolutely nothing, never thinking they should assist. George Floyd was cuffed and on the ground, yet they claimed he tried to resist. Eight minutes and forty six seconds, Derek Chauvin used to send him on his way. No my people, this was not God's will, the devil didn't let him stay. A bit of white foam on the side of Floyd's mouth and blood releasing from his nose, Chauvin looked at the small crowd of blacks as if to say, 'This is how it goes'. Even when I watched the video I wanted to make a gesture. I thought, 'This could have been my brothers; Bruce, Allen, or Lester'. George Floyd was a man crying for his deceased mother. You watched it; he wasn't a white man of course, he was yet another brother. We wonder why the racist officers continue to do what they do. Even though we have signs in our hands and yelling "Black Lives Matter Too". Perhaps they know they have the go ahead from the racist Commander who we see. So, if it's left to the racist cops, black men will never be free. I believe the majority of black men would love to say, 'Peace be still'. But will somebody tell me how, when they're being killed at will?" In the month of November come out like we did for forty four; our President Barack. We don't have to get our hair did and we can wear dirty kicks and one sock. Yes, we should always look our best and yes we should always smell good. But we should never ever do this in place of peacefully defending our hood. I know we may want Chauvin to burn like white bread becoming burnt toast. But when we're burning down our homes, I have to admit we're doing the most. A peaceful protest we should hold, let's act like we have some sense. Then we could show the world that we have class and we'll surprise Trump and Pence. George Floyd was a Daddy to Gianna who carries years of six. So Derek Chauvin didn't just kill him, he threw his baby in the mix. "My Daddy changed the world" she said, with two long ponytails tied. But Gianna wants her Mommy to tell her how her Daddy died. She held her little GiGi close with an expression that said,

'No'. I understand if she didn't tell her, because that's no way to go. His friends called Floyd a Gentle Giant, and resistance was never made. I know that it will never bring him back, but I hope his family gets paid. Please don't ever forget his murder, and don't throw his name in the dump. As I write I'm sitting here wondering who will be next to sit next to Crump. Chauvin was happy when using one knee, if he could he would have used the two. With evil he applied his strongest pressure as if he had nothing better to do. Chauvin's knee or Kaepernick's? Which would you like to see? Chauvin used his to murder, Kaepernick so murder wouldn't be. Well, at least the punk is in jail right now and he has to stay in the Shoe. He'll never be safe in the general population where some inmates will kill and shout. Since this is the case I wanna say to the warden, 'I'll pay you if you let him out'. Chauvin should have been given to Floyd's family and gotten whatever he got. If there was any breath left in him, he should have been given that shot. But before they put him on the table I'd like to hear him call for his mother. I'd like him to hear Eric Garner in his head saying, 'This is for killing another brother'. It hurt my heart to watch Philonis uncontrollably cry as he tried to explain to CNN how he felt watching his older brother die. He said he just had to watch it, he had to see it for himself. And now it will take forever and a day to place that memory on the shelf. Never again will he see his big brother walking this earth and alive. Instead he has to figure out just how he'll continue to survive. He was his older brother whom he will always love. But now he has to talk to him from the Earth looking above. I am so sorry, Mr. Floyd; you didn't deserve what you received. Had I not seen it with my very own eyes I don't think I would have believed. Needless to say when I watched you die, I was angry, I was mad, and I was hot. All I could repeatedly say to myself was, 'Derek Chauvin deserves to rot'. The only positive you gained from this is that you're once again with your mother. Share how you screamed for her while being killed because you were a brother. You can also tell your Momma that you didn't know if the the bill was fake; all you wanted were cigarettes, but murder's what you were forced to take. In tears I know you'll tell your Momma that you can't forget how you were treated. With cuffs on your wrists and no way to breathe, all you could do was be defeated. I know she'll immediately hold you tight as you described how you were very pained. Then she'll tell you to follow her so she could show you the wings you gained. At least eighteen rotten complaints against Derek Chavin were made. But the department seemed to ignore the stench; instead, they covered it with glade. Two people in a car chase died, and this involved Chauvin too. Several murders on his hands which he believed he had the right to do. All I can say to you, Mr. Floyd is this: 'I'm happy the foam is now gone and I'm happy your nose is now dry. But it saddens me now to know that your family had to say goodbye. I'm happy that your neck is now free and I'm happy your oxygen's back too. Regarding your little GiGi, I wish there was something I could do. Rest easy Mr. Floyd; all the pain is gone. And now you are forever free, not just maybe until dawn. And I'm glad you're not alone up there, you're surrounded by love of your mother's. I'm also glad that you're surrounded by all the other murdered brothers. For a long time many will be angry, and for a long time many will cry. But I hope your family knows that one day you'll meet them in the sky.

END OF CHAPTER 16

The Master Told Them He Was Nice

(The Elders Meet Tamir Rice)

At the conclusion of Big Mike's rap performance, sad faces were shared all around. Everyone was left speechless with enough tears to make a mound. The silence in the Greater Room was anything but that. The very loud cries of the brothers showed just where their hearts were at. The brothers cried profusely; George wailing from anger so great. He didn't understand how any human being could demonstrate such hate. Tamir looked a bit confused but even he knew what the rap meant. On earth he loved to hear hip-hop music but now he wondered how he was sent. Amadou seemed to calm down the fastest and he created a circle with his brothers. He decided to place George in the middle as the story was his and no others'. The remaining brothers locked arms and Amadou began a sway. From side to side the brothers moved and Amadou had something to say. As the circle remained unbroken, the brothers' shoulders swayed to an unheard beat. Then Amadou suddenly told them that he had something for them to repeat. Without the movement of the brothers ceasing, he explained what he wanted them to do. He looked at the colors of his brothers and began his chant, "Black Lives Mattered Too. Black Lives Mattered Too". Initially very low, the brothers' voices' climbed to decibels of ten. After each sway, Big Mike's rap was remembered so the brothers swayed again and again. "Black Lives Mattered Too. Black Lives Mattered Too". Even Tamir joined in the chat, quickly learning what to do. In the midst of the circle George stood in a bit of confusion not knowing who was who. Shaking his head one time or two, he remembered what his brothers were told to do. Still feeling angry, the tears began to allow the skin on his face to dry. But with every beat of his heart, George continued to ask himself, "Why"? Amadou put an end to the chant and allowed the circle to be unbroken. He told the brothers to gather around George and not a word was to be spoken. With bowed heads and eyes closed, the thoughts of the brothers were not the same. But Amadou whispered his thought to himself: "Those racist pigs thought they were playing a game". Breaking the silence amongst the brothers, it was Trayvon who gained the courage to first speak. "Is it okay if I sit back at the table for a minute? I'm feeling kinda weak". The brothers not only obliged his request but thought it was best for all of them to do. While at the table George looked at his brothers and thought, "Now I know who is who". When he opened his mouth to speak, it seemed his imprisoned words were free. "Thank you my brothers", he said. "Thank you for loving me". The responses from his brothers were all at once given, and George was thankful that once again he was in the land of the living. Having not forgotten, Trayvon reminded the elders that they hadn't heard Tamir's story yet. Lowering his head and picking it up again, it was Tamir's face that now appeared wet. Nervously he remembered who he was among and slowly said, "Okay, I'll go". Trayvon reminded him that his introduction didn't have to rhyme and he could go slow. Tamir cleared his throat in a nervous preparation to speak about his life on Earth. Trayvon knew that whatever he heard, his youngest brother's life would have had some worth. "Remember we're your brothers", Trayvon said. "We're here and we gotcha back. If you stutter a bit or forget your words, don't worry we'll give you some slack". The other brothers nodded their heads to confirm that they agreed. Almost instantly Tamir began to speak, confident that their help he wouldn't need. And he began:

"Well, I'll tell you guys what I remember. I lived in Ohio with my Mommy and I think I had one sister who was a little older than me. I don't remember if I had more sisters and brothers and I can't remember if I had a Daddy. I liked to play a lot of sports like basketball, football, and soccer and oh, I almost forgot; I like swimming too. I had a whole bunch of toys but my favorite one was my toy gun. It was my favorite because I liked to play cops and robbers with my friends and my cousin. Plus my toy gun was so soft and I liked the way it felt when I squeezed it in my hand. My Mommy bought it for me and she said I could play with it whenever I wanted. I didn't live in like a real good neighborhood so my Mommy made sure that my toy gun didn't look real because she didn't want anybody to think it was real and hurt me. You could tell it wasn't real because it wasn't big like the guns that cops had. My gun had bright orange squishy stuff around the top and it had some in the back too. I liked to play outside with my toy gun and sometimes I played all by myself. I remember that I used to go to the Cudell Recreation Center that was in the park. I liked to go in there a lot because it was a lot of fun. They had a arts and crafts program and I was one of the kids that went there. I um, um, um, um, I did things like sculpting and pottery and crocheting and stuff. I always made stuff for my Mommy there and I used to surprise her when I gave it to her. So anyway I um, I um, I was was playing outside near the park where the Recreation Center was. I was playing by myself with my toy gun. It was so cool. I saw some police and they were running real fast like they were chasing somebody but I didn't see anybody else running in front of them. Then all of a sudden the police started yelling at ME for no reason. I didn't really know what they were saying because they were yelling and they were all yelling at the same time. I remember that um, um, um, um, um, I was playing by myself and I wasn't doing nothing bad. I wasn't doing nothing wrong. I was just playing with my favorite toy gun. And then all of a sudden I saw the police running to ME and then I saw them holding their REAL guns. So then the next thing I know I heard their guns shoot. And the next thing I know my chest started hurting real bad and I fell on the ground. Then I was dizzy and um, um, um. I was dizzy and I couldn't see that good because everything was blurry. Then I remember I was hearing a lot of yelling and I saw my sister running to me and her hand was like reaching for me when I was on the ground. Then, next thing I know I seen the police throw

A CONVERSATION BETWEEN THE BROTHERS

my sister on the ground for no reason and then they put some handcuffs on her and she was crying real bad. And I remember that I was still laying on the ground for like um, um, um, I don't know how many minutes? And I was seeing a lot of people around me but nobody was touching me and helping me get up or nothing. And I was on the ground for a really really long time and then I heard some sirens and then they picked me up and put me on this bed thingy and I don't know but I think I was going for a ride. Then I kinda remember going to a hospital and a lot of people was next to me? And the Doctors or the Nurses I don't remember. They kept giving me shots. I hate shots but anyway um, um, um, then they was yelling too and everything was still blurry, and then I got real sleepy, and then I went to sleep. And I don't remember nothin' after that". Tamir took a deep breath at the end of his last sentence, glad to be done. Again the tears stung the brothers' eyes and Amadou whispered to himself, "Again the racist cops won". Eric began snapping his fingers near one of his ears as if he was trying to think. The snaps came faster and louder as his eyes refused to blink. "What is it Eric?", George asked. "What are you trying to remember?" "Tamir's introduction sounds familiar", he responded, "And I believe it happened in December. I was still alive on Earth then and it's coming back to me now. You were the kid that happened to? It was you, little brother? Wow"! Eric quickly stood up from the table as if he had something to do. He turned and looked at Tamir and said, "I can clear some things up for you. All of your introduction was true, but there's more to your story too". He looked at his brothers and asked, "Would you guys mind if I tell y'all more stuff that happened? I promise I'll be real quick". The brothers gladly gave him permission because the air in the Greater Room was now thick. And Eric began:

"Like I said, I remember this happened sometime in December. I remember 'cause it was cold outside. I was wearing my skier's mask on my face because it was the coldness of the wind I tried to hide. Yes little bro, you were living in Ohio; Cleveland to be exact. After you were shot, it took the ambulance four whole minutes until you were tracked. But I'm kinda gettin' ahead of myself so let me slow down and chill. Like they did me, racist cops murdered you on the spot, the only difference is mine took longer and I wasn't shot. I don't remember the last name of the white punk but I know his first name was Timothy. It was obvious that you were an innocent kid but they killed you like you were the enemy. Like you said, your toy gun had orange stuff on it; anybody could see it was fake. But as they usually do, the racist cops shot anyway and then claimed it was a mistake. The dude who called 911 even reported that your gun was probably fake and that you were probably a juvenile. The two officers claimed that they NEVER received this information; not just later or a while. Now there are bad kids everywhere, but not you little bro, you was straight. Your Mother raised you to love everybody. You ain't know nothin' 'bout hate. 'A pleasant young man', that's how they described you at your school. You took your education seriously; you had it on the cap, you was no fool. Now like you said, you ain't run from the cops 'cause you ain't do nothing wrong. They were always takin' black brothers' lives and that day they took you along. Now that dude said your gun was fake in the beginning of the call and in the middle. I believe those racist pigs knew it, but ignored it like it was a riddle. When they saw that you were black, they knew what they would do; shoot you and say it was self defense. But you was a kid playin' with your fake gun, so everybody knew that ain't make no sense. Now somebody tell me how a squishy orange gun and a black steel gun could ever look the same. And another thing I do remember is that the cop's excuse was lame. He had the nerve to say that he told you to show him your hands, but instead you tried to draw a gun. Nah how in the hell they couldn't see you was just a kid playin' in a park not even tryna run? Timothy claimed he knew it was a gun when you reached in your pocket and he saw it coming out. Now anybody with good sense should've known that that was a lie without a doubt. But anyway, Timothy was the one who shot you. He shot you one time in your chest. He didn't know and he didn't care that he was murdering one of the best. The reason you remember being on the ground long is because it took four minutes for help or the FBI to arrive. You didn't even live that far away, but they didn't rush to keep you alive. Maybe it was because they knew where they had to go and what people lived there; I don't know. But the racist cops who were already there could've helped you though. They said they didn't know what to do but that's CPR 101. But nah, they ain't give a damn 'cause they saw you as just someone's black son. You're right, your sister was older than you by two years; she was fourteen. You saw her hand reaching out to you 'cause she knew what was done to you was mean. She was screamin' and cryin', tryna get to you to help her little brother. Those pigs were so foul that later that day they threatened to arrest your mother. Now this was because she got extremely upset when they told her what happened to you. She took it so hard she couldn't calm down, but if you was their son, they would've been that way too. By the way you were right, they did cuff your sister and throw her on the ground. Those punks did this because she wanted to help you, so they didn't want her around.   Not only did they handcuff and tackle her to the ground, they put her in a patrol car too. All because she wanted to do what they wouldn't; she tried to save you. I can't even imagine how she felt looking through the window watching you slip away. Locked in there, cuffed behind her back, having nothing she could do or say. But they didn't care, they saw her as just another older sister to a younger black sister. To them she was just another angry black woman who they needed out of their hair. But she was a loving older sister to her brother at whom she could only stare. Oh wait a minute, lemme back up. I don't remember the first name of the second cop, but I know his last name was Barnback. There wasn't a lot being said about him 'cause he wasn't the one who shot the young black. But in my opinion, he was guilty by association and he didn't restrain Timothy nor hold him back. Now wait a second, where was I at? Your murder is still in my head. I'll never forget the thought of a little boy shot and laying on the ground for dead. But anyway, lemme get back to where I was.   I was talking about Barnback. He shoulda been seen as the shooter too; he should notta been given no slack. I'm sure your sister thought you would die on the ground that day, but you actually died the next. And how dare they threaten to arrest your mom; this would make any parent vexed.   You said you were in the hospital, that's true, they were tryna give you the best of care. Now in my opinion if the racist cops couldn't, someone from the precinct shoulda been there. Even if they weren't seen by your family at least they woulda shown they had a heart. See, this just proves what I've been trying to say: they were guilty from the start. Aight, I'm tryna wind this down, I know I said I wouldn't be long. It's just when I even talk about this mess, my anger gets so strong. But anyway little bruh, your family sued Cleveland, those racist cops, and got six mill. I'm sure it was just the principle of the matter 'cause you are back here still. Anyway, black lives mattered and those cops were outta pocket. They shoulda been thrown into a tiny cold cell and your family allowed to lock it. Now check this out, listen y'all: the racist cops got off good. When it first went down they got a slap on the wrist and everybody knew they would.   Their guns were taken away, they were taken off the streets, but stayed in the precinct still getting paid. That was probably 'cause they wanted to make sure no contact with your family was made. Eventually the racist pigs got off in court too. It was ruled that their actions were justified, meaning it was okay for them to shoot you. Now check this out, this is the kicka: There was an investigation after two years. So what, your family was still shedding tears.   Before Timothy worked in the urban section, he worked in the suburban section of the city.   I'm guessing that once the investigation started, it got down to the nitty-gritty. Turned out when Timothy worked in the suburbs he was deemed an emotionally unstable recruit. But this was one year after your family won in court and settled their lawsuit. Timothy knew he was, so on his application he made sure it didn't show. When the urban section found out about it, they told him he's got to go. How we used to say it? 'Ya ain't gotta go home, but you gotta leave here'. And that's what happened too. When this was discovered, Little Timmy's ass was outta there! But The Cleveland Police Department was wrong too 'cause they never checked his file. If they did they would've easily seen that he had issues for a while. Anyway, I don't know why ole Tim Tim thought that eventually he wouldn't get caught. I mean what in the Hell was he thinkin'? Mannnn, just like my Auntie used to say: 'He shoulda been shot with shit and killed for stinkin'. People aroun' the world were talking about you, not just black people but white. I mean even my man Stevie Wonder coulda seen that shit just wasn't right. Anyway, I hope I cleared that up for you Little Bruh, and I'm sorry that happened to you. Like I said before, I heard about your story on earth, but us being brothers? THAT I never knew". At the end of his clarification speech Eric gave Tamir a hug and told him he was proud to be his Brother From Another Mother. "When did I get up here?" Tamir asked, "Was that when I went to sleep?" Eric knew that homecoming feeling all so well, so he answered "yes", then started to weep.

END OF CHAPTER 17

It's Better Out Than In

(Black Lives Matter And Win)

All at once the brothers heard the sound which they'd heard so many times before. Each one quickly eyed the other before they all turned towards the door. The Master was returning to them but this time they didn't know why. Secretly, they hope that whatever the reason, it wouldn't again make them cry. The Master entered The Greater Room wearing a never before seen Dashiki colored gray. The brothers assumed that after one wear, he threw them all away. The Master greeted His sons, but told them He hadn't come to stay. There was another room within the University that he wanted to show them that day. The five brothers turned to look at Amadou as if he'd been holding out. The Master knowingly assured them that even Amadou knew not what this was about. He asked His sons to follow Him as He swiftly walked this and that way. Amadou asked the Master how long it would take them to get there. The Master responded, "Remember my son, everyday is everyday". The others also wanted to know how long, to where, as well as why. But instead they took comfort in knowing that it was somewhere within the University's sky. Before what the brothers deemed wasn't long, they were in another mansion, so beautiful to see. Tamir couldn't believe his childish eyes and thought, "Is this all for little ole me"? The Master opened the very heavy amethyst door without any strain at all. Once inside He showed them around and at last they arrived at a wall. The Master touched the wall and immediately there was an unfamiliar glow on His face. The wall opened when He released His hand and revealed a vast space. Had Amadou and Trayvon were to describe it, the closest would be the mansion where they'd watched Spike's show. They continued to follow the Master as He told them the way that He would go. The Master's tour ended in a room with a glass encased movie screen. But it was unlike those that the brothers had on earth; this size had never been seen. The Master welcomed them to sit in the area which held the Maserati chairs. They obliged and when they did, they REALLY had no cares. As they allowed their bodies to melt within their seats, the Master began to talk. As soon as He began to speak, Amadou hoped he wouldn't hear, "Now my sons, it's time to walk". Instead, the Master began to tell them why the room was built. He started by saying that within the room they should feel no guilt. He told them that when He built this room, He named it "The Theater Of Mental Revenge". In the room they'd create their very own movies about their murderers and all the brothers' avenge. They would not feel guilt or regret at what they decided to create. Whatever they felt would give them mental comfort, they did not have to abate. He reminded them that each of them had his own story to be told. And a clear and stable mind is worth more than the University's grounds of gold. The brothers looked around at each other and wondered who would start. Already knowing what they thought, the Master said, "I'll let you guys decide that part. I'll leave you here my sons, until you feel your work has been done. And if you want to know the limit you'll have to visit this room, my answer is 'There is none'". He reminded the brothers of where the areas that held the food were. In a sound of more than jubilation, Tamir's voice said, "Yes Sir"! The Master knew they'd still be hard to find because the mansion was so large. With trust in his first son who arrived he said, "Amadou, I'm putting you in charge". Before He turned to walk away, He said to his sons, "I thirst". They knew that the Master would return to them, so they started deciding who would create first. As they did, they enjoyed the speeds of their chairs and how they could move fast or slow. Feeling comfortable and confident, Brother George raised his hands and said, "I'll go". George remembered that he didn't have to write his movie; it could be vocally dictated. He told his brothers that he'd try to dictate his creative story in a rhyme in tribute to their "Name Game", but he wasn't making any promises. He used the lessons that the Master gave him and the screen created what he verbally dictated:

"HOW WILL YOU FEEL WHEN YOU MEET THE BROWNS?" (A SHORT STORY FOR DEREK CHAUVIN)

"Face down on concrete slab, white foam on the right side of his mouth, and blood releasing from his nose. Now, I'm not sure this is what happened, but I'm hoping this is how it goes. The straps are so tight around his neck; this time it's he who screams "I can't breathe". The black Executioner brings in his colleagues; four men who looked like him. And just like him, all four colleagues took an oath to assist. He pulls the neck strap tighter 'cause he thought he saw Derek Chauvin resist. "Get off the table Chauvin, let's see how well you fight". "I can't, I can't, I can't; the straps around my neck are too tight. 'Ah, Ah, Ah' he screams at the same time that he's crying. One of the colleagues mimics him as if he was a baby whining.

The racist Chauvin thinks to himself that living is starting to look grim. Then it hit him that he killed George Floyd and he'd die a similar death as him. The four colleagues continued to stare as if this was a good reality based movie. Chauvin's right eye begged for help from them; but nope, that's where they were and that's where they'd stay until the movie ended: eight minutes and forty six seconds after start time.

When he could, he opened his eyes, but suddenly they closed. He thought he saw a sea of brown, so still as if it was posed. But then he thought he was losing his mind and maybe this is how one dies. He tried to repent for all of his murders, and he tried to repent for all of his lies. With the foam on the right side of his mouth, and the red blood releasing from his nose, he thought to himself, 'I can no longer speak; it's already too late I suppose'.

The executioner turned to get the syringe while his colleagues called Chauvin a "clown". He managed to turn his head to the left, but he definitely couldn't turn it aroun'. His left eye was completely pressed against the concrete slab. But with his right eye barely working, he thought, 'Again I see that brown'. Finally giving up, Chauvin thought, 'I guess I'm on my own'. His right eye darted again and this time he saw a large glass. Although the sea was larger, there were heads on top of that brown. As if to try to guess what this was, he closed the right eye tightly and opened it back. Still very drowsy with little oxygen left, he thought he saw a very large and clear bag. Chauvin wanted the injection and thought, 'It has to be better than this'. He really didn't want to die at all, his friends and family he would miss. Unbelievably, he saw that the "melting pot of browns" changed to shades of the same: Very light, light, medium and dark. Realizing that he was certainly going to die, he cried out loud for his dead mother. With tears flowing from his right eye, he thought he saw the Browns with sticks. And then he thought, 'I don't wanna die, my precious Cody just turned six'. Now noticing that the Browns had separated with two sticks on each side, Chauvin nervously thought to himself, 'I think I've already died'. But he seemed to get a second wind and wondered where that shot was at. The right eye then saw hands holding signs that read, "Nah, you ain't' going like that". Now the Executioner stood with his four black colleagues; hands behind him and still. Chauvin surprisingly thought, 'Could this all be God's will'? The right eye saw that each of the Browns had laughing expressions on their face. Knowing again that he'd be dead, he thought

'I wish God would just send me some grace'. The black Executioner and his black colleagues seemed to be laughing too. And all the punk could do was take it; there was nothing he could do. Chauvin's oxygen levels dropped and the beat of his racist heart dropped lower. He thought, 'This is my last chance to find out what's behind that glass'. The glass slid to the side so that Chauvin's right eye could get the best look at the Browns. They were now moving, and the signs were now blank. The racist punk saw above the Browns, the beautiful sky so blue. The murdered brothers then flipped their signs:

"BLACK LIVES MATTERED TOO"

Derek Chauvin died immediately after meeting the murdered brothers. But immediately before he took his last breath he thought, 'I never wanted to see those thugs and hoodlums again. For crying out loud, that's why we murdered them in the first place. Thank God I won't see them in the University; they won't be there for sure'". His right eye joined the left and together they closed in death. Just as it was in their reality, the murdered brothers already knew it would take some time for the African American Team to remove Chauvin from the concrete slab. They would have to wait for the Doctor to come in to pronounce the punk dead. Although they knew themselves that "Chauvin The Knee Punk" was already dead, "Team Black" refused to release the restraints from his body. They agreed that they would keep them there for eight minutes and forty six seconds after he was pronounced dead. After an hour of waiting, the brothers agreed that the reason the "Pronouncer" was taking so long was because he had six floors of black men whom he had to pronounce dead first. Knowing this, the brothers went to the vending machine for popcorn and a drink. Upon their return, they agreed that they would not eat the popcorn nor enjoy the drink until they experienced the feeling that would come over them when they saw Derek Chauvin's body for the very last time. At last the "Death Pronouncer" was there and the brothers started opening their bags of popcorn as he laid the stethoscope on the left side of Chauvin's chest. As the stethoscope was moved to the right, the brothers agreed that their mouths were watering so badly. They wanted to eat their popcorn! The "Racist White Cop Turned Death Pronouncer" looked at his watch and informed the Executioner of the "time of death" Chauvin would take with him to his forever home called "The Lake Of Fire". The murdered brothers watched as "Team Black" grabbed the "Murder Assisted Straps" and reluctantly released them from the body of the punk. In agreement, "Team Black" allowed the hand straps to remain as they were the closest to the representation of the handcuffs that I was made to wear while I was being murdered by the now dead "Chauvin The Knee Punk". The handcuffs stayed in place for twelve minutes: Six minutes for the age of my beautiful GiGi, and just for good measure, six more for the precious little Cody who had just turned six. They saved the neck strap for last; they had previously agreed that it should remain there for another eight minutes and forty six seconds; just because they felt like it. Once that was done and in revenge, they snatched his carcass and together dragged him from the concrete slab onto the dirtiest gurney the colleague had found. Once on the gurney, "Team Black" slowly rolled the punk to the left and towards the elevator. Each of the brothers had already placed a handful of white cheddar cheese popcorn near the right side of his mouth and a can of fruit punch towards his nose. As they talked about the gaul that Mr. Punk had when he thought that he wouldn't see them in the University, the black Executioner (who suddenly grew "human wings") arrived at the elevator and pushed the button for.......... DOWN! While watching the Chauvin carcass entering the elevator and the elevator closing, the brothers sighed and in unison, shouted, 'It's done"! Again in unison, they placed the hand which held the white popcorn to the right side of their mouths and slowly allowed it to touch their tongues as they took "Human Bites". They chewed and enjoyed the taste for eight minutes and forty six seconds before they swallowed. Next, they popped the top and held the red fruit punch can towards their noses and into their mouths. They were saddened to notice that their red was going in but mine had gone out. They did not discard their now empty popcorn bags and red fruit punch cans. Instead, they kept them as a tribute to me when they'd have the very unfortunate pleasure of meeting me too soon at the University. Knowing that there was nothing they could do except meet me when I returned to the University, the brothers stood as one by one they placed their signs in the large unused plastic bag which they'd brought with them just in case their stomach fluids wouldn't be able to stay where they belonged. One by one they arrived at the University's Welcome Gate where they were greeted by the Master. Suddenly, I remember that when the Master first welcomed me, we took an elevator to my first area of introduction. Once in the elevator, the Master pushed the button for.......... UP.

My Epilogue: After he declared "Derek Chauvin The Knee Punk" dead, the Pronouncer hurriedly walked out of that room and headed to the

Emergency Room. They had already told him that he would be needed there. The entire right side of the Emergency Room held many more black men who needed to be pronounced. I was one of them. He already knew that I was a high profiled case. He was therefore on time restraints because he'd have to run to the bank to withdraw the money. He knew he had to pay the Medical Examiner for his autopsy results on behalf of the police department and Washington. Transfer given and promise stated, the Pronouncer continued declaring dead, all of the African American men who laid lifeless as a result of several racist whites . After two hours, he thought he'd rest before continuing this bunch because he knew more men of color killed by racist cops would be arriving soon. This meant more trips to the bank for him. As soon as he pulled out his chair to sit, he heard the specialized ringtone. It was coming from his private cell phone. On the other end was the Medical Examiner who spoke only two words: 'It's done'. The Pronouncer kept this phone out and made two calls: one to the Police Precinct and one to Washington. To each he simply played the old school game we played back in the day: "Telephone". To each person, he passed on the two words from the Medical Examiner who started their game: 'It's done'. He then put his private phone in his pant's pocket and the business phone in the pocket of his dingy lab coat. He walked back to the ER to continue his permission to one by one, send the black men off to the University or the Lake of Fire; Didn't matter to him". George and his brothers jumped from their Maserati chairs and hugged each other in disbelief. The movie confirmed that the Master was wise because great was their relief. Amadou's face wore a hatred smirk when remembering Chauvin calling his brother a "clown". Then he remembered when he saw "The Lake Of Fire", he took an elevator where the Master pressed the button for…….. DOWN!

END OF CHAPTER 18

Don't Believe What You Heard

(The Master Travels with A Black Angel Bird)

The brothers heard a very loud bell, but it was different from the welcome chime. Very pleasant to their ears, it rang more than just one time. Not long after, they saw the Master come in wearing clothes which Giorgio Armani could never design. In fact, without each other knowing, all of them thought, "Armani should now resign". But there was something else different about the Master; He carried a large bird on His shoulder. Unlike any of the earthly birds, this bird seemed older and bolder. Without knowing why, the brothers rose as if the Master was a great king without a crown. They knew they'd never done this before and the Master said, "No, please sit down". He explained that He had to take a trip down to Earth with his angel bird. Tamir looked at the Master as if confused and replied, " Angel Master? Is that what I heard"? "Yes my son, there are many here and I always take one with me when I go". Still confused, Tamir asked, "Aren't angels supposed to be white"? The Master chuckled and said, "My son, I know you were taught this on earth, but now you need to know it wasn't right. Earth has wrongfully and mistakenly taught you that black is evil, bad luck, or mean. And that is why Timothy felt comfortable shooting you on site at the scene. 'If you're black, stay back; if you're brown, you can hang around, but ohhhhhh, if you're white'? 'Then most certainly you're ALL RIGHT!' I did not create the Earth that way, but some down there are stubborn and refuse to see the light. This black bird is certainly an Angel and as you've heard, her songs are as lovely as can be. You all will learn a lot about blacks because when I return I'll have someone with me". "How will you get there?" Tamir asked. "Will you fly on a special broom stick"? Trayvon answered, "There are many cars we can choose to ride but the beautiful chariots we cannot pick". Amadou responded, "Very good, little brother, you can tell him why". "The Master only uses them to bring home the sick who die. He can easily get to earth because the chariots can fly." Tamir asked, "But Master, why do you take an angel with you when you go? That's the part I don't know". "All of you have seen angels after you died. You don't remember because they hid; not wanting you to know they cried. I must escort my angel bird to Earth and chauffeur my sick who have died. As I've said, the one who returns with me will teach you a lot about blacks. He's black himself, very knowledgeable, and has a very good heart. We need to go, murdered black men crowd the skies, so we should get a headstart". Black Angel on his shoulder, He turned and walked away. Although the brothers stared at one another, no one knew what to say. Tamir broke the ice by asking Trayvon who he thought was coming back. "We don't know, but we have to trust the Master. The Master said he's black. While the Master and His Angel were gone, the brothers talked amongst themselves. They also visited the Book Room where black authors filled the shelves. James Baldwin, Zora Neal Hurston, Alice Walker, Langston Hughes, Maya Angelo, Richard Wright, Ralph Ellison, and Octavia Butler. These were just a few. Amadou had a thought come to mind, so he knew what he would do. He'd teach his brothers a similar game while they waited for the Master. He hoped they'd all have fun and perhaps feel time move just a bit faster. Each brother had to choose Authors and name the titles of their books in a rhyme. The brothers accepted the challenge and they agreed they had some time. Trayvon encouraged Tamir by telling him he'd help him out. Because he now trusted his brother, he knew he would without a doubt. The game was such a hit that the brothers played through their meals. They learned as they played so they felt like they'd gone shopping and caught some deals. Before they knew it, they were playing as they talked about the return of the Master. Since every day was every day, Amadou remembered time couldn't move faster. As if on cue the brothers heard a very large bell; similar to the welcome chime. Once again, they discussed amongst themselves what it could mean. Though anxious and suspicious, they continued their newly found game of black books. Some of them spoke about honest people while others portrayed crooks. Even yet again, the brothers stopped playing when suddenly beautiful notes rang. This time they recognized the pleasant sound; it was that which the Master's Black Angel Bird sang. The brothers knew someone had arrived when some time later they recognized other sounds. They were the same as the ones they made when walking on the University's gold grounds. They hadn't met anyone else in the wing where they now sat. All of them knew that the Master had returned and all were nervously glad about that. They waited and listened as the gold ground's sounds came closer to their ears. Amadou and Trayvon didn't know why, but they started shedding tears. At once the brothers watched the Master walking towards them with a stranger. They had no fear at all because at the University there was no danger. The man who walked beside the Master was dressed in a dark suit and tie. They wanted the reason for that last bell sounding, and now they finally knew why. Just as the Master told them he would be, the man was in fact black. He walked without fear or trepidation, so the brothers were taken aback by that. The man appeared much older than they; He was bald but in his hand he carried a hat. There was a tiny square shaped metal pin on the lapel of his left chest. As the Master and the man came even closer, the brothers felt less distressed. In a whisper they asked who he could be and what illness he'd had. Just as they were when they returned home, they hoped the man was glad. While pondering if he was the Master's successor, they heard the Master say, "Arise my sons". He extended his hand towards the man and said, "Meet John R. Lewis; THE PROFESSOR".

THE END

About the Bio

TRACY E. HUMPHREY dreamed of becoming a published author. SHE DID IT thanks to GOD, husband; The Honorable Judge Wayne A. Humphrey, "Patty Cakes","Mommy" (Imani Bolling), Dawn Barrett, Dr. Burcescu, Dr. Lang, and Ms. Eartha B. Williams and Pastor Cousin. Tracy resides in Westchester County, New York with her loving husband, and sons; Greyson and Tony.

Interested In Writing and/or Publishing a Book?

Visit Dr. Synovia @a2zbookspulishing.net

Printed by Libri Plureos GmbH in Hamburg, Germany